# POWER *and* PLACE:
## INDIAN EDUCATION
## IN AMERICA

BY VINE DELORIA, JR.,
& DANIEL WILDCAT

*American Indian Graduate Center*
and

FULCRUM
GOLDEN, COLORADO

Library of Congress Cataloging-in-Publication Data

Deloria, Vine.
  Power and place : Indian education in America / Vine Deloria, Jr., and Daniel Wildcat.
    p. cm.
Includes bibliographical references and index.
  ISBN 1-55591-859-X (pbk.)
  1. Indians of North America—Education. 2. Education and state—United States. 3. Indian students—Government policy—United
States. 4. United States—Social policy. I. Wildcat, Daniel. II. Title.
  E97 .D47 2001
  371.829'97—dc21
                                                    2001001721

Portions of this book were first published
in *Winds of Change* magazine

Book design: Pauline Brown, Pebble Graphics

Cover illustration and design © 2001 Kayeri Akweks

Cover images: Courtesy of the Cumberland County Historical Society, Carlisle, Pennsylvania. The same Navajo group is pictured in 1882—before (top image) and after (bottom image) entering the Carlisle Indian School.

Printed in the United States of America
0 9 8 7 6 5

Fulcrum Publishing
4690 Table Mountain Dr., Ste. 100
Golden, Colorado 80403
(800) 992-2908 • (303) 277-1623
www.fulcrumbooks.com

## BOOKS BY VINE DELORIA, JR.

*Behind the Trail of Broken Treaties: An Indian Declaration of Independence*

*Custer Died for Your Sins: An Indian Manifesto*

*God Is Red: A Native View of Religion*

*The Metaphysics of Existence*

*Red Earth, White Lies: Native Americans and the Myth of Scientific Fact*

*Spirit and Reason: The Vine Deloria, Jr., Reader*

# CONTENTS

*by Vine Deloria, Jr.*

Formal Indian education in America stretches all the way from reservation preschools in rural Native communities to prestigious urban universities far away from Indian cultural centers. The educational journey of modern Indian people is one spanning two distinct value systems and worldviews. It is an adventure in which the Native American sacred view must inevitably encounter the material and pragmatic focus of the larger American society. In that meeting ground lies an opportunity for the two cultures to both teach and learn from each other.

*Power and Place* examines the issues facing Native American students as they progress from grade school through college and on into the professions. Subject matter as diverse as the school systems of the Five Civilized Tribes in the early 1800s to what Albert Einstein's theory of relativity *really* means is found on these pages. Native people navigating American systems of higher education must absorb a great deal of factual content, and they must also place that knowledge into the context of their own tribal and community traditions. For American Indian students the scientific method and the Western worldview coexist with Native spirituality and a deep connection with the earth.

This collection of fifteen essays on Indian Education is at once philosophic, practical, and visionary. Beginning with an essay on American Indian metaphysics and progressing to a bold, uplifting scenario for an Indian future grounded in education, *Power and Place* offers a concise reference for administrators, educators, students, and community leaders involved with Indian education.

# PRELUDE TO A DIALOGUE

*by Daniel Wildcat*

Let's begin with the big picture, because at the most basic level that is precisely what Vine Deloria, Jr., addresses in *Power and Place*. Those familiar with Deloria's work over the last four decades know his appraisal of why we, Indians, are still such a problem for America's dominant social institutions—for example, religion, politics, education, economics, and so on. In short, we do not fit comfortably or conveniently within Western civilization. This is not a regret. It is an affirmation—a living testimony to the resilience of American Indian cultures. If there is another group of people in America who have faced all the forces this society and its government could bring to bear in destroying their identity and fundamentally reshaping them in the image of the dominant society, I would like to meet them. Consequently, these essays are a criticism of the formal and official institutions of Indian education. Additionally, and more importantly, I believe, they constitute an explicit effort to open discussion about what a truly American Indian or what I would call an *indigenized,* educational practice would look like.

This book is proposing nothing less than an indigenization of our educational system. By *indigenization* I mean the act of making our educational philosophy, pedagogy, and system our own, making the effort to explicitly explore ways of knowing and systems of knowledge that have been actively repressed for five centuries. Make no mistake about it, what Deloria is proposing is radical and exciting. *Power and Place* introduces an agenda for much hard work—intellectual, social, and political—that can only be accomplished within institutions that we build based on our own indigenous North American insights and, most fundamentally, metaphysics.

# American Indian
# Metaphysics

*V. Deloria*

A Prelude to Understanding
Indian Education

For many centuries whites scorned the knowledge of American Indians, regarding whatever the people said as gross, savage superstition and insisting that their own view of the world, a complex mixture of folklore, religious doctrine, and Greek natural sciences, was the highest intellectual achievement of our species. This posture of arrogance produced some classic chapters in the history of the Western Hemisphere: Ponce de Leon wandering around the southeastern United States vainly searching for the fountain of youth, Swedish immigrants on the Delaware River importing food for thirty years because they could not grow anything in this country, and the Donner Party resorting to cannibalism because of their fear of the local Indians.

In recent years there has been an awakening to the fact that Indian tribes possessed considerable knowledge about the natural world. Unfortunately, much of this appreciation has come too late to enable anyone, white or Indian, to recapture some of the most important information on the lands, plants, and animals of the continent. In a parallel but unrelated development, Indian religious traditions are now of major interest to whites, whose own religious traditions have either vanished or been swamped in reactionary fundamentalism. Fluctuating between a recognition of Indians' practical knowledge about the world and outright admiration for their sense of the religious is unsettling and nonproductive; it does not attribute to Indians any consistency, nor does it suggest that their views of the natural world and religious reality had any more correspondence and compatibility than do Western religion and its science. Instead of talking of an Indian "science" or even an Indian "religion," we should focus our attention on the metaphysics possessed by most American Indian tribes and derive from this central perspective the information and beliefs that naturally flowed from it.

Metaphysics has had a difficult time regaining its intellectual respectability in Western circles. Its conclusions were greatly abused by generations of Europeans who committed what Alfred North Whitehead called the "fallacy of misplaced concreteness," which is to say that, after they reached the conclusions to which their premises had led them, they came to believe they had accurately described ultimate reality. Metaphysics need not bear the burden of its past, however, if we understand it as simply that set of first principles we must possess in order to make sense of the world in which we live. In this sense the Indian knowledge of the natural world, of the human world, and of whatever realities exist beyond our senses has a consistency that far surpasses anything devised by Western civilization.

The best description of Indian metaphysics was the realization that the world, and all its possible experiences, constituted a social reality, a fabric of life in which everything had the possibility of intimate knowing relationships because, ultimately, everything was related. This world was a unified world, a far cry from the disjointed sterile and emotionless world painted by Western science. Even though we can translate the realities of the Indian social world into concepts familiar to us from the Western scientific context, such as space, time, and energy, we must surrender most of the meaning in the Indian world when we do so. The Indian world can be said to consist of two basic experiential dimensions that, taken together, provided a sufficient means of making sense of the world. These two concepts were place and power, the latter perhaps better defined as spiritual power or life force. Familiarity with the personality of objects and entities of the natural world enabled Indians to discern immediately where each living being had its proper place and what kinds of experiences that place allowed, encouraged, and suggested. And knowing places enabled people to relate to the living entities inhabiting it.

Western scientists frequently suggest that the Indian way of looking at the world lacked precision because it was neither capable of nor interested in creating abstract concepts or using mathematical descriptions of nature. But, as Carl Jung pointed out with respect to the so-called primitive mind, once a person knew the places of things, a mere glance was sufficient to replace counting and, in most instances, was more accurate. The Indian mind was considerably more interested in learning the psychological characteristics of things than in describing their morphological structure. Hence, in some instances when defining common personality traits that people and animals shared, the Indian seemed to be talking nonsense. He or she appeared to be combining aspects of things that, at first glance, could not and should not be together. Today, as Western science edges ever closer to acknowledging the intangible, spiritual quality of matter and the intelligence of animals, the Indian view appears increasingly more sophisticated.

Indian students today are confronted with the monolith of Western science when they leave the reservation to attend college. In most introductory courses their culture and traditions are derided as mere remnants of a superstitious, stone-age mentality that could not understand or distinguish between the simplest of propositions. Additionally, they are taught that science is an objective and precise task performed by specialists who carefully weigh the propositions that come before them. Nothing could be further from the truth. Western science traditionally represents the consensus of the established scientists who almost always reject new ideas out of hand and spend their time gathering evidence to bolster outmoded paradigms. Much of the progress made by Western science has been made by amateurs and martyrs who have been disparaged and cursed in their lifetime, only to be canonized by a new generation that has learned to accept the smallest of changes with more grace than their parents and teachers.

Indian students are further misled by outrageous claims made by science, which suggest that the various fields of inquiry, if taken together, represent the sum total of human knowledge. In fact, almost all of Western science is reductionist in nature and seeks to force natural experience and knowledge into predetermined categories that ultimately fail to describe or explain anything. The whole process of Western science is that of finding common denominators that can describe large amounts of data in the most general terms, rejecting anything that refuses easy classification as "anomalous," existing outside the generally accepted labels and, therefore, not to be given standing or serious attention. This way of gathering information about the world—and ourselves—is, of course, absurd.

One of the most painful experiences for American Indian students is to come into conflict with the teachings of science that purport to explain phenomena already explained by tribal knowledge and tradition. The assumption of the Western educational system is that the information dispensed by colleges is always correct, and that the beliefs and teachings of the tribe are always wrong. Rarely is this the case. The teachings of the tribe are almost always more complete, but they are oriented toward a far greater understanding of reality than is scientific knowledge. And precise tribal knowledge almost always has a better predictability factor than does modern science, which generally operates in sophisticated tautologies that seek only to confirm preexisting identities.

We live in an industrial, technological world in which a knowledge of science is often the key to employment, and in many cases is essential to understanding how the larger society views and uses the natural world, including, unfortunately, people and animals. Western science has no moral basis and is entirely incapable of resolving human problems except by the device of making humans act more and more like machines. Therefore, Indian students, as they study science and engineering, should take time and make the effort to regain a firm knowledge of traditional tribal lore. Even if many of the stories seem impossible under existing scientific explanation of phenomena, Indian students should not easily discard what their tribes have traditionally believed. There is most assuredly a profound knowledge present in many things that the tribes have preserved.

Richard Ford's article "Science in Native America" is a good representative piece recognizing the knowledge of Indians. It fairly surveys the various aspects of knowledge that Indians had and gives reasonable explanations of some of the ways in which our ancestors understood natural phenomena. Considering the present state of things, it is important for scholars such as Ford to begin to help us break the ice of ignorance and neglect that has been thrust upon our traditions for more than half a millennium. Without the voices of respected white scholars, there is little chance that we can get sufficient attention from the scientific establishment in order to plead our own case. But we must remember that every article attempting to discuss this problem should be understood as a call for each of us to enter into the exchange of knowledge. In this sense, Ford calls us as Native Americans to become more truly scientific—to offer our knowledge to the larger benefit of our species.

We must not, however, rely on the assistance of sympathetic non-Indian thinkers for guidance, as they often do not see the kinds of relationships that traditional Indian knowledge reveals. The current tendency of younger Indian scholars is to find where the tangent points exist with Western science and to proclaim, quite rightly, that Indians arrived at the same conclusions using a much different epistemology or metaphysics. Recognizing these points where communication is possible is but halfway to the goal. We may grant that the energy described by quantum physics appears to be identical to the mysterious power that almost all tribes accepted as the primary constituent of the universe. But what does this conclusion say about the theories of disease, powers of spiritual leaders, or interspecies communications with sympathetic birds and animals? Surely when we reach these conclusions we should see more clearly how Indians then accommodated their ways of living to this knowledge.

Most adventures in metaphysics attempt to fix upon a few basic concepts and, using these abstract ideas, explain the remainder of the experiential world in those terms. Indians use a peculiar way of maintaining a metaphysical stance that can best be termed as "suspended judgment." People did not feel it obligatory that they reach a logical conclusion or that they could summarize the world of experience in a few words and sentences. Black Elk, after telling John Neihardt the story of the reception of the sacred Pipe, said, "Whether it happened so or not, I do not know. But if you think about it, you will see that it is true." The hallmark of the true Indian philosopher was the ability to hold in suspended judgment the experiences he or she had enjoyed or was told, and to file away that bit of knowledge until the time when more data of closely related content came his or her way.

Indian students, therefore, should consider themselves to be standing in the shoes of their grandparents as metaphysicians. While specific answers are required within the context of Western science, we should remember that these answers are only a temporary statement that is subject to rejection or further refinement at any time. If the non-Indian or even Indian teacher or professor absolutely insists that a certain conclusion is true, remember the grievous sin of the Western mind: misplaced concreteness—the desire to absolutize what are but tenuous conclusions. Students should further remember that while the Indian knowledge is designed to relate to other kinds of experience and knowledge, Western science does not necessarily form a unity. In the reduction of knowledge of phenomena to a sterile, abstract concept, much is lost that cannot be retrieved. By maintaining the personal involvement typical of wise Indian elders, the students should be able to maintain themselves as practical and competent metaphysicians.

# INDIGENIZING EDUCATION: PLAYING TO OUR STRENGTHS

*D. Wildcat*

*Power and Place* constitutes a declaration of American Indian intellectual sovereignty and self-determination. It is essentially a tribal intellectual and moral mandate requiring action, unless we want our current educational system to be like our contemporary political structures and practices, which all too often merely reflect the dominant society's institutions. Consequently, the decision to begin a discussion of American Indian education with a consideration of metaphysics is challenging and well-founded.

Even a cursory examination of the numerous problems facing modern technological societies and the failure of modern education systems to find solutions to these problems, which are essentially moral and ethical in character, suggests something is fundamentally amiss in the dominant education systems of the United States. The conflict between Western science and religion, and the inability of the vast majority of Western thinkers to find a common ground or consistent intellectual framework, speak directly to the central problem with Western metaphysics: the failure to produce a coherent worldview encompassing the processes of the world and how we humans find meaning in those processes.

The late Carl Sagan recognized this problem in his posthumously published work *Billions and Billions: Thoughts on Life and Death at the Brink of the Millennium.* Sagan described and reported on the truce or, I am tempted to say, treaty, reached between Western science and religion. But his and other scientists' immersion in

Western metaphysics, as indicated in their appeal "Preserving and Cherishing the Earth: An Appeal for Joint Commitment in Science and Religion," is symptomatic of the schizophrenic nature of Western metaphysics. American Indians know from experience that forming an alliance or making a treaty does not address irreconcilable differences in worldviews. Furthermore, such an alliance is of little help if the problems of the earth are largely exacerbated by both the Western institution of religion and that of science, as Deloria has persuasively argued in *God Is Red, The Metaphysics of Modern Existence*, and most recently in *Spirit and Reason*.

The institutions of Western science and religion are like partners in a dysfunctional marriage: caught up in a relationship of codependency. The good news is that within both institutions some individuals and groups are seeking changes. Especially in science, a whole new generation of researchers is moving from long-standing scientific models or theories (to be discussed shortly) to approaches for understanding the world that sound increasingly like the wisdom conveyed in many traditional American Indian stories, ceremonies, and practices. There are some affinities or convergences between cutting-edge Western science—for example, Cajete's *Look to the Mountain*, Suzuki's *Wisdom of the Elders*, and Thomas's *Tribe of Tiger* to name a few—and traditional experiential knowledge, or what has recently been called traditional ecological knowledge. Increasing evidence suggests that there are good reasons for American Indian students not to discard knowledge traditionally held by their tribes—knowledge at once ecological, moral, practical, and most certainly philosophical. The very fact that these words or categories were not used to describe this knowledge tells us a great deal about holistic thinking, its sources, and the kinds of knowledge such thinking produces.

## WHAT MUST CHANGE

This book is for teachers, parents, students, and leaders who recognize that something of great value existed in the "old ways." We must not romanticize the past—everything was not perfect. But if we want to truly exercise self-determination, there is no better place to start than with an effort to give our children an inheritance too many generations of American Indians were outright denied or have struggled mightily to maintain: identity within tribal cultures we were actively engaged in, as opposed to existence within a culture of indoctrination facilitated most effectively through U.S. government education programs.

It is critical to understand that Deloria's essays are not primarily about raising standards or improving test scores; rather they constitute a reasonable call to consider the advantages of building an educational practice on a foundation of American Indian metaphysics that "is a unified worldview acknowledging a complex totality in the world both physical and spiritual." This undertaking will not be easy, and we do need allies.

There is much work to be done and need for serious dialogue in comparing what is described as the Western metaphysics of space, time, and energy to the American Indian metaphysics of place and power. A true dialogue is long overdue. With respect to morality, the dialogue is easily started with the explicit rejection of what archconservative William Bennett has called the need to fix or find the "moral compass." Beginning a dialogue with a map, so to speak, of Western civilization's metaphysical landscape is critical, for it is distorted and consequently its moral compass is askew. Unlike William Bennett's reformist solution to the problems facing American education—going back to the core values of Western civilization—Deloria argues that the very tradition and system of knowledge Bennett wants Americans reconnected to is actually the problem. Consequently, we must begin a discussion of education in America with the metaphysical assumptions of Western civilization implicit in and underlying modern notions of curriculum and pedagogy, given that so little attention is paid to the topic today.

The problem with Indian education in America is really the problem of education in America, regardless of whether recipients of the education are, figuratively speaking, red, yellow, black, or white. Of course, the historically racist character of American education cannot and should not be minimized. Rather the point ought to be made that the early formulation of Indian education, as articulated by its architects, should have been seen as the "miner's canary," warning of problems with the underlying assumptions implicit in Western civilization and its system of education.

For all of the fuss about innovation in educational methods, curriculum, and pedagogy today, it is worth noting that, with respect to higher education, the basic organization of the institution, the division of subjects, and teaching methods have changed little since the establishment of the first colleges and universities in Europe during the twelfth and thirteenth centuries. Curriculum, at all levels of American education, bears the largest imprint of Western metaphysics. It is easy to see the influence of Aristotle's categorizing of experience and knowledge at work in how we divide and teach subjects. The medieval division of the seven liberal arts into the trivium (grammar, logic, and rhetoric) and the quadrivium (geometry, astronomy, arithmetic, and music) conforms with Aristotle's philosophic division of subjects. The natural sciences, as we now recognize them, were not added until the eighteenth and nineteenth centuries. Aristotle's legacy within Western metaphysics, especially as it continues to shape Western notions of education, cannot be underestimated.

Higher education in America is one of the most conservative Western cultural institutions in America. The fact that obtaining a higher education is a widely accepted goal in America suggests that elementary, middle, and secondary schools are critical in preparing students to succeed in an institution more representative of Western metaphysics than any other. Therefore, the hope for American Indian education lies first in the explicit identification of features of the Western tradition or worldview that produce many of the problems we are immersed in today; and second, in the active reconstruction of indigenous metaphysical systems, which, I believe, result in experiential systems of learning.

WESTERN SCIENCE: MATERIALISM
AND MACHINE METAPHYSICS

The first task can be accomplished by articulating the main features of the Western tradition and then counterpoising key features of

American Indian or indigenous North American metaphysics. For example, most of science, continues to reduce reality to a physical world. Consequently, knowledge itself becomes reduced to generalizable principles by which atoms, genes, or "things" appear to act. The method of inquiry, the methodology of science, is reduced to essentially taking things apart—dissection, whether on a lab table or in a controlled experiment. In spite of new research in the areas of ecology, complexity, the phenomenon of chaos, the process of emergence, and much of cutting-edge physics, science as taught in most schools is reductionist—in terms of what counts as reality, knowledge, and the appropriate methods for acquiring knowledge.

If one doubts this characterization, one need only look at the talented ecologist E. O. Wilson's commentary for the sesquicentennial of the American Association for the Advancement of Science, "Integrated Science and the Coming Century of the Environment." Wilson reduces life itself to genetic mechanisms, although this reductionism does not keep him from concluding, "The unavoidable compliment of reductionism is synthesis." But a synthesis at what level, based on what metaphysical assumptions? Wilson's answer is clear: a unified system of knowledge in the natural and social sciences as well as the humanities will be integrated at the level of biology and chemistry. The problem of understanding life is merely a question of measurement, of developing the tools (technology) for unlocking the mysteries of life found in the microscopic particles (parts or pieces) of genes, and telescopic exploration into the birth of galaxies. The popular and published works of Wilson and neo-Darwinist Richard Dawkins, of *The Selfish Gene* fame, suggest the humanities, the social sciences, and psychology itself are reducible to chemical and biological, in other words, genetic structure.

Another complementary and lingering feature of Western thought, albeit one increasingly under attack, is the idea of the world as machine. The mechanistic worldview continues to be applied to many of the physical sciences and biology and, as stated above, very quickly results in a methodology that is essentially dissective in character. Proponents of this "popular mechanics" view of the world in the biological and physical sciences share an optimistic faith in the belief that once the instruments and tools (technology) are developed that will allow us to observe and measure the smallest pieces of the world, that is, genetic codes and subatomic particles, we will be able to understand the world. This view is strangely "comforting" to all who strive to arrive at objective knowledge by taking their selves out of the picture, so to speak, by avoiding our own selves' emotions and feelings, attachments and dislikes, which arguably determine more of our everyday lives in the world than biochemical processes identified in laboratories.

Let's be clear: certain "things" can be understood using the metaphysics of time, space, and energy. However, a great deal of what we experience cannot be explained within the metaphysics of Western science, and that is the critical point. An entire realm of *human experience in the world* is marginalized, declared unknowable, and, consequently, left out of serious consideration. This reality cannot fit in the objective experimental box of mechanical cause and effect, and no tool or technology will change this situation unless we merely say that all there really is to the world is mechanics (in the structural sense) and tools. Western notions of reality and corresponding ideas of knowledge are not far from this cold "scientific" assessment.

INDIGENOUS METAPHYSICS

Compare the scientific worldview to widely shared tribal views in which humans understand themselves to be but one small part of an immense complex living system, something like Lovelock's Gaia Hypothesis. This hypothesis offers a holistic worldview in the most profound sense, where attention to relations and processes is much more important, at least initially, than attention to the parts of our experience. The point should be obvious: we, human beings, in all our rich diversity, are intimately connected and related to, in fact dependent on, the other living beings, land, air, and water of the earth's biosphere. Our continued existence as part of the biology of the planet is inextricably bound up with the existence and welfare of the other living beings and places of the earth: beings and places, understood as persons possessing power, not objects.

Traditional American Indian cultural practices actively acknowledge and engage the power that permeates the many persons of the earth in places recognized as sacred not by human proclamation or declaration, but by experience in those places. And it is experience that shapes indigenous education and necessitates the awareness of self as crucial in order for knowledge to be attained. In American Indian metaphysics, unlike the dominant system of Western metaphysics, awareness of one's self is the beginning of learning, and it certainly precedes the times most of us can think back to or remember. Child and cognitive psychologists now agree that most of the learning we do as human beings happens before we are five years old. A study of child development from an indigenous standpoint would lead to insights that popular causal models cannot. Deloria's formulation that power and place equal personality is ripe for exploration in the study of human development.

Among so much sadness and dysfunctionality in our world today, it is at once sobering and energizing to think of what we might accomplish by giving our children something our parents and grandparents stubbornly held on to but were never given the opportunity to openly embrace: a way of living that found lessons on humility, generosity, and hope in the world—hope not for something in the distant future but hope in the sense of acting with the confidence and expectation that something good will happen. Ask any child psychologist—such a condition is not romantic, but crucial for the full development of healthy adults.

A good deal of the ills surrounding us today are the fault of a society where children learn life lessons that make their formal education often seem meaningless. After all, most of what we know is *not* a result of explicit pedagogy or teaching; it is learned through living. Many human beings seem so caught up in their machines and technology that they have forgotten or lost the very real sense of what it means to live: to make choices that enrich life as opposed to making existence more comfortable.

Science has accomplished much in the latter case and, as Deloria notes, little in the former case: "Western science has no moral basis and is entirely incapable of resolving human problems except by the device of making humans act more and more like machines." "Making humans act more and more like machines"—this may be the most modern of reductionisms. It also explicitly illustrates an increasingly impoverished notion of experience and reality, and one that, thankfully, increasing numbers of human beings are questioning. It is hard to understand something if one is always controlling and taking it apart.

Fortunately, a growing number of modern ecologists, environmental scientists, biological scientists, and geographers now readily accept the wisdom that Chief Seattle spoke to nearly 150 years ago: "We are all related ... whatever befalls the earth befalls man." The concepts of the food chain, ecosystem management, population dynamics, and a host of cycling processes are, at one level, scientific expressions of the traditional American Indian wisdom Chief Seattle spoke to so eloquently. At this easily observable and documentable level, science seems to be moving closer to traditional American Indian wisdom.

At the most fundamental level this interconnectedness and relatedness of human beings to the earth provides the first principle for our rich spirituality. A spirituality that is literally grounded in our experience of the natural world as full of creation's power; a spirituality that denies the dichotomies that most often define Western religions. This is not romanticism; it is acknowledgment of a living people's experience, and something science too often anesthetizes its students and practitioners to.

PLAYING TO OUR STRENGTHS

It is at the level of experience that our traditional and ancestral indigenous scholars have left us the richest legacy—insights of the processual, interconnected, and interrelated nature of the phenomenal world; insights too often precluded by indoctrination in the metaphysics of Western science and, more generally, the modern Western worldview. At the heart of *Power and Place* is the suggestion that before we all become specialized mechanics of different aspects of the phenomenal (so-called objective) world, we seriously explore and attempt to recollect a way of knowing where interpretation or meaning (subjective) is integrated in the realm or reality of experience.

Few thinkers have written about the objective-versus-subjective and nature-versus-human dichotomies of Western thought as perceptively as Alan Watts, a scholar of Eastern thought, in the introduction to his book *Nature, Man, and Woman*. Watts notes that Western humankind's faith in intelligence has led many to "think we know" how the world works, and consequently, to presume we have some right to control the organization of life itself. He states:

> This is an astonishing jump to conclusions for a being who knows so little about himself, and who will even admit that such sciences of the intelligence as psychology and neurology are not beyond the stage of preliminary dabbling. For if we do not know even how we manage to be conscious and intelligent, it is most rash to assume that we know what the role of conscious intelligence will be, and still more that it is competent to order the world. (p. 2)

In Western thought scientific theories of reality, knowledge, and methods for knowing are logically consistent. The problem is that they constrain, even preclude, any discussion of our human experience and life as a part of processes involving power(s), which are irreducible to discrete objects or things.

CONVERGENCES

There is reason to be cautiously optimistic. The relatively new concept of emergence as used in ecology and physics may capture how personality, as defined by Deloria, develops in specific places possessing power. Emergence refers to a model of change or development where change is not reducible to a discrete factor or factors, but rather the interaction of multiple factors or causes that are understood as processual in character as opposed to mechanical. I am of the opinion, as are a number of scholars and scientists, both indigenous and nonindigenous, that when everything is said and done the concepts of complexity, self-organization, ecology, and even evolution (as reformulated in primarily a space-dependent process as opposed to a time-dependent model) are actually ideas that are part of ancient indigenous intellectual traditions in North America. I like to tell modern nonindigenous scientists that I am glad to see that their modern science is finally catching up with very ancient indigenous wisdom. This at least always gets their attention! Although philosophers of science have pointed out various problems with the dominant Western view and a fair number of scientists would acknowledge those problems, the vast majority still do science the old-fashioned way. As my Salish friend Jaune Quick-To-See-Smith summarizes, Western scientists theorize a hypothesis (a cause and effect), design an experimental process—which is by design far removed from the world we live in—and produce a result or a finding that too often is then understood as "fact."

Nevertheless, the worldview or paradigm shift now underway in cutting-edge physics (chaos theory, nonlinear models of development and change) and biology (complexity, emergent properties, bio- and phytoremediation, etc.) is predicated on the recognition that the old Western metaphysics on which science was built results in certain kinds of knowledge, but not all knowledge. Most important, the old Western metaphysics of time, space, and energy never allows one to get the "big picture" of the world. The essays in this book are advocating a holistic worldview, one resulting from experience in the earth's living systems. Ultimately, *Power and Place* advocates big-picture worldviews containing metaphysical systems that, most significantly, integrate the physical and spiritual dimensions Western civilization presents as opposed to each other.

American Indians are natural systems thinkers, as Indian entrepreneur Rebecca Adamson has remarked, because even today many American Indians seem to intuitively perceive the interrelatedness of problems and recognize that solutions required to solve them must be holistic in nature. The strong affinity or convergence between what I call the new complex view of science and American Indian metaphysical traditions is worth exploring; both are at odds with the old mechanical and naive physical views of the world. At a certain point it seems the phenomenal world was bound to assert its presence on what might best be described as Western intellectual asceticism—that is theoretical abstraction disconnected from experience in the world.

INDIGENOUS LIFE LESSONS

*God Is Red* was the first book to really trace the deep roots of the ongoing conflict between Western civilization and American Indian worldviews to the Judeo-Christian tradition and its overwhelming influence on Western thought. It seems reasonable today to question whether Western science itself has unconsciously carried a considerable amount of baggage from its early roots in religious institutions. Simply think of the degree to which theory, paradigm, and model construction in Western science and, sadly, in education itself, develop not based on—but in spite of—human experience and worldly evidence, and the historical extrapolation from religious asceticism to scientific asceticism seems appropriate.

The ultimate irony for the followers of Enlightenment ideals of liberty, reason, and justice is that the rationality they have most fully developed is of a mechanical and technical nature. The practices and products of Western science have, intentionally or not, had the net effect of making "humans act more and more like machines," and why should we be surprised? All of the genuine enthusiasm for the final mapping of the human genome is an ex post facto demonstration of the extent to which modern science is preoccupied with mechanics. If life itself is viewed mechanically, why should humans be any exception?

Welcome to the brave new world—not Huxley's book, but the citadels of contemporary DNA science. Orwell's *1984* had it half right: Big Brother need not worry about watching you, nor you worry about being watched by Big Brother. So long as He is sure you are watching him. Imagine the influence of a culture that induces members to passively watch—the news, advertisements, and TV sitcoms. We do indeed live in an industrial, technological world, and many of us have now reached the place where it seems important to ask why so many suffer emotionally, economically, physically, and spiritually. Education ought not be reduced to mechanics. Today we must play to our strengths. Indeed, what we need are indigenous life lessons, and that is what *Power and Place* explores: indigenous life lessons emergent from experience in the world.

## BEGINNING AN HONEST DIALOGUE

It is easy to criticize any system of thought or culture, especially the less direct experience one has of the lives of the people possessing those ideas or that culture. I hope these essays will not be read as a bashing of Western civilization, but rather as the beginning of a long-overdue honest dialogue. With respect to culture, a person can have only the most superficial understanding of a people, especially their culture, if it is based primarily on the written word and only limited direct experience of their everyday lives. It is not surprising, therefore, that with only a few exceptions members of the larger, essentially Western, or immigrant, American culture have great difficulty understanding American Indian or indigenous North American peoples and their cultures.

Of course when the same logic is applied and the circumstances are reversed, most American Indians are better prepared to understand and critique the Western tradition because they, like it or not, have had a five-centuries-long history of being pushed and pulled into the dominant culture, although the culture they experienced in the boarding schools could hardly be called normal or ordinary—even by Western standards. Indeed, the legacy of government and parochial boarding-school experiences explains a significant degree of the dysfunctionality found in American Indian institutions, communities, and homes and has also unintentionally formed the catalyst for some of the most hopeful developments to emerge for American Indians in the last half century.

Today most American Indians, such as they have received a formal education and, until very recently, employment, have done so in the context of Western-inspired institutions. Amazingly some have been able to hold on to many of their indigenous tribal beliefs, values, and practices alive within their Native communities and reservations. The general point is that American Indian educators, in particular, unlike their non-Native counterparts, are better prepared and well suited by experience to critically look at the deep roots of Western-inspired institutions and practices. Because of their bi- and often multicultural experience we can and should explore creative ideas and ways of establishing healthier Indian communities and sovereign Indian nations.

Let us go even a step further. If "we talk and you listen," as Deloria suggested three decades ago, non-Natives might even learn something useful. Indigenous people obviously have benefited from some of the technological innovations developed by Western scientists. Unfortunately, the arrogance or faith instilled by Western civilization's claim to ownership of Universal Truth has, until now, dissuaded Americans from seriously listening to what American Indians have to say. Their loss is, I believe, great.

For those non-Indians who choose to listen, the following is intended as an invitation to discussion, even exploration of some ground literally and figuratively, seldom covered today. Few adults in the United States learn and work in institutions formed on principles outside of or distinct from Western civilization; this includes most American Indians. Almost all Indian education studies, reports, and commissions have described, analyzed, and bemoaned a Western-inspired institution built on curriculum, methodologies, and pedagogy consistent with the Western worldview. This much-studied educational system was and, sadly, remains too often directed toward cultural assimilation into the dominant society. Fortunately, some American Indians still live and understand the world indigenously. Circumstances—political, economic, technological, and spiritual—have brought many in America today to places where a reintroduction or resurgence of Indian education in America can seriously be entertained. We have come to places in modern industrial and postindustrial societies where experiences are suggesting we might have valuable lessons to learn by exploring what once existed throughout this hemisphere: indigenous education systems.

# POWER AND PLACE
# EQUAL PERSONALITY

*V. Deloria*

Western science resolves itself into certain "laws" that describe the natural world. These laws are makeshift descriptions of the manner in which physical reality appears to operate, but they are often regarded by Western scientists as inviolable. Phenomena that fall outside the prescribed patterns of behavior are said to be "anomalies," which can be disregarded when explaining how the physical universe functions. Eventually, of course, the Western scientist must deal with the so-called anomalies. These phenomena form an increasingly large body of knowledge and facts that cannot be explained using the acceptable paradigm into which the rest of scientific knowledge is deposited.

American Indian knowledge of the world does not suffer this structural handicap. While tribal peoples did not have a detailed conception of the whole planet in the sense that Western scientists presently do, they did have a very accurate knowledge of the lands they inhabited and the plants, animals, and other life-forms that shared their environment. It is also becoming increasingly clear that they had a fairly comprehensive knowledge of the heavens, with their own sets of constellations and stories.

The boundaries of American Indian knowledge were those of respect, not of orthodoxy. For instance, certain stories about the stars could not be told when the constellations in question were overhead. Some other kinds of stories involving animals, plants, and spirits could only be told at a particular time of year or in a specific place. There were no anomalies because Indians retained the ability to wonder at the behavior of nature, and they remembered even the most abstruse things with the hope that one day the relationship of these things to existing knowledge would become clear.

The key to understanding Indian knowledge of the world is to remember that the emphasis was on the particular, not on general laws and explanations of how things worked. Consequently, when we hear the elders tell about things, we must remember that they are basically reporting on their experiences or on the experiences of their elders. Indians as a rule do not try to bring existing bits of knowledge into categories and rubrics that can be used to do further investigation and experimentation with nature. The Indian system requires a prodigious memory and a willingness to remain humble in spite of one's great knowledge.

Although the rank-and-file professors may reject this rather cumbersome method of obtaining knowledge, it has been recognized by some important thinkers as being equal to the reductionist procedure. Percy W. Bridgman, one of the giants in physics in this century, made this remark in his book *The Way Things Are:*

> I may have observed all men, including Socrates, and found that they were mortal, and summarized by researches in the statement "all men are mortal," which I then filed away in my mind for future use. Later when I may have forgotten all the details of my former research, I may find a rational basis for charging Socrates for annuity which I am selling him, and my assurance that Socrates is mortal, which I get from my mental file, guides me in setting my price. The syllogism thus has economic value for me in this situation. The unlettered American Indian, however, confronted by the same situation, would doubtless meet it by recalling that he had once verified that Socrates in particular was mortal. (p. 91)

So we have different paths to the same conclusions.

Keeping the particular in mind as the ultimate reference point of Indian knowledge, we can pass into a discussion of some of the principles of the Indian forms of knowledge. Here power and place are dominant concepts—power being the living energy that inhabits and/or composes the universe, and place being the relationship of things to each other. It is much easier, in discussing Indian principles, to put these basic ideas into a simple equation: Power and place produce personality. This equation simply means that the universe is alive, but it also contains within it the very important suggestion that the universe is personal and, therefore, must be approached in a personal manner. And this insight holds true because Indians are interested in the particular, which of necessity must be personal and incapable of expansion and projection to hold true universally.

The personal nature of the universe demands that each and every entity in it seek and sustain personal relationships. Here, the Indian theory of relativity is much more comprehensive than the corresponding theory articulated by Einstein and his fellow scientists. The broader Indian idea of relationship, in a universe that is very personal and particular, suggests that all relationships have a moral content. For that reason, Indian knowledge of the universe was never separated from other sacred knowledge about ultimate spiritual realities.

The spiritual aspect of knowledge about the world taught the people that relationships must not be left incomplete. There are many stories about how the world came to be, and the common themes running through them are the completion of relationships and the determination of how this world should function. Such tales seem far removed from the considerations of science, particularly as Indian students are taught science in today's universities. However, when the tribal concepts are translated into scientific language, they make a good deal of sense. Completing the relationship focuses the individual's attention on the results of his or her actions. Thus, the Indian people were concerned about the products of what they did, and they sought to anticipate and consider all possible effects of their actions.

And on Appropriateness

The corresponding question faced by American Indians when contemplating action is whether or not the proposed action is appropriate. Appropriateness includes the moral dimension of respect for the part of nature that will be used or affected in our action. Thus, killing an animal or catching a fish involved paying respect to the species and the individual animal or fish that such action had disturbed. Harvesting plants also involved paying respect to the plants. These actions were necessary because of the recognition that the universe was built upon constructive and cooperative relationships that had to be maintained. Thus, ceremonies such as the First Salmon and Buffalo Dance and the Strawberry Festivals and the Corn Dances celebrated and completed relationships properly or ensured their continuance for future generations.

We can view this different perspective in yet another way that will speak more directly to Indian students studying Western science. Very early, at least beginning with Greek speculation on the nature of the world, the Western peoples seemed to have accepted a strange binary system of reasoning in which things are compared primarily according to their size and shape. Out of this perspective came the natural sciences as we have them today. Eventually distinctions were made primarily on the basis of shape, and from this tendency came the great theory of evolution that now reigns in the West. All our knowledge of the natural world within the Western framework derives from a crude comparison between skeletons of animals. Very little knowledge exists about the animals themselves except relative bone structures. We only speculate on how they see the world, think, and understand emotional experiences. Increasingly, studies show them to have as complete an emotional/intellectual life as we do.

American Indians seem to have considered this kind of thinking at one time because there are tribal stories comparing humans to various animals. The stories always emphasized that while humans cannot see as well as hawks, they can see; they are not as strong as the bear, but they are strong; not as fast as the deer, but they can run; and so forth. However, when these comparisons are carefully analyzed, one finds that both physical and psychological characteristics are described. Indians derived their knowledge of birds and animals from actual experiences, and therefore physical structure meant little to them as they anticipated encountering these creatures in the future and needed to know how they behaved for hunting and protection purposes. Thus Charles Eastman was taught that when approached by a bear or mountain lion, one should pick up a stick immediately so that the animal would think he was armed and dangerous.

When using plants as both medicines and foods, Indians were very careful to use the plant appropriately. By maintaining the integrity of the plant within the relationship, Indians discovered many important facts about the natural world that non-Indians only came upon later. The Senecas, for example, knew that corn, squash, and beans were the three Sisters of the Earth, and because they had a place in the world and were compatible spirits, the Indians always planted them together. Only recently have non-Indians, after decades of laboratory research, discovered that the three plants make a natural nitrogen cycle that keeps land fertile and productive.

Plants, because they have their own life cycles, taught Indians about time. George Will and George Hyde, in their book *Corn Among the Indians of the Upper Missouri*, point out that it was the practice of the agricultural tribes to plant their corn, hoe it a few times, and then depart for the western mountains on their summer buffalo hunt. When a certain plant in the west began to change its color, the hunters knew it was time to return home to harvest their corn. This knowledge about corn and the manner in which its growth cycle correlated with that of the plants of the mountains some 500 miles away was very sophisticated and involved the idea of time as something more complex than mere chronology. Time was also growth of all beings toward maturity.

STAR KNOWLEDGE

Much Indian knowledge involved the technique of reproducing the cosmos in miniature and invoking spiritual change, which would be followed by physical change. Hardly a tribe exists that did not construct its dwellings after some particular model of the universe. The principle involved was that whatever is above must be reflected below. This principle enabled the people to correlate their actions with the larger movements of the universe. Wherever possible the larger cosmos was represented and reproduced to provide a context in which ceremonies could occur. Thus, people did not feel alone; they participated in cosmic rhythms.

Star knowledge was among the most secretive and sophisticated of all the information that the Indians possessed. Today archeoastronomers are finding all kinds of correlations between Indian practices and modern astronomical knowledge. Very complex star maps painted on buckskin hides or chiseled on canyon walls give evidence that Indians were astute observers of the heavens, and their ceremonial activities were often based on the movement of the heavens. A good deal of Indian star knowledge continues to exist, but religious prohibitions and restrictions still limit the propagation of this information. Some star knowledge goes very far back into the past when the sky looked different. The Sioux said there was once a bright star in the middle of the Big Dipper. Today we can suggest that a black hole does properly exist there.

## THE PRINCIPLE OF CORRELATION

Star knowledge gives us an additional principle of Indian information gathering. That principle is correspondence, or correlation. Being interested in the psychological behavior of things in the world and attributing personality to all things, Indians began to observe and remember how and when things happened together. The result was that they made connections between things that had no sequential relationships. There was, consequently, no firm belief in cause and effect, which plays such an important role in Western science and thinking. But Indians were well aware that when a certain sequence of things began, certain other elements or events would also occur.

A kind of predictability was present in Indian knowledge of the natural world. Many ceremonies that are used to find things, heal, or predict the future rely upon this kind of correlation between and among entities in the world. The so-called medicine powers and medicine bundles represented this kind of correlative under-standing of how different things were related to each other. Corre-lation is responsible, for example, for designating the bear as a medicine animal, owls as forecasting death or illness, and snakes as anticipating thunderstorms.

This kind of knowledge is both tribal- and environmental-specific. In diagnosing illness, for example, medicine people might search for the cause of sickness by questioning their patients on a variety of apparently unrelated experiences. They would be search-ing for the linkages that experience had taught them existed in these situations. Here again, there was considerable emphasis on the heavens. One need only examine the admonitions of different tribes with respect to shooting stars, different configurations of the moon, eclipses, and unusual cloud formations to understand how correlational knowledge provided unique ways of adjusting to the natural world.

## A More Realistic Knowledge

The Indian method of observation produces a more realistic knowl-edge in the sense that, given the anticipated customary course of events, the Indian knowledge can predict what will probably occur. Western science seeks to harness nature to perform certain tasks. But there are limited resources in the natural world, and artificial and wasteful use depletes the resources more rapidly than would otherwise occur naturally. The acknowledgment that power and place produce personality means not only that the natural world is personal but that its perceived relationships are always ethical. For that reason, Indian accumulation of information is directly opposed to the Western scientific method of investigation, because it is pri-marily observation. Indians look for messages in nature, but they do not force nature to perform functions that it does not naturally do.

Indian students can expect to have a certain amount of diffi-culty in adjusting to the scientific way of doing things. They will most certainly miss the Indian concern with ethical questions and the sense of being personally involved in the functioning of the natural world. But they can overcome this feeling and bring to science a great variety of insights about the world derived from their own tribal backgrounds and traditions. They must always keep in mind that traditional knowledge of their people was derived from centuries, perhaps millennia, of experience. Thus, stories that seem incredible when compared with scientific findings may indeed represent that unique event that occurs once a century and is not likely to be repeated. Western knowledge, on the other hand, is so well controlled by doctrine that it often denies experiences that could provide important data for consideration.

By adopting the old Indian concern with the products of actions, students can get a much better perspective on what they are doing and how best to accomplish their goals. By maintaining a continuing respect for the beliefs and practices of their tribes, students can begin to see the world through the eyes of their ancestors and translate the best knowledge of the world into acceptable modern scientific terminology.

Most important, however, are the contributions being made by American Indian scientists. With their expertise, we can better frame our own ethical and religious concerns and make more constructive choices in the use of existing Indian physical and human resources. It is this linkage between science and the community that we must nurture and encourage. We must carry the message that the universe is indeed a personal one. It may, indeed, be a spiritual universe that has taken on physical form and not a universe of matter that has accidentally produced personality.

# UNDERSTANDING THE CRISIS
# IN AMERICAN EDUCATION

*D. Wildcat*

Maybe we do live in an information age. In fact, it would seem reasonable to say we are witnessing an information revolution, and as heretical as this may sound, it may be a large part of the most disturbing problems we see surrounding us today. The so-called Information Highway may be a curious phenomenon, but it is amazing that almost no one stops to inquire as to where it is taking us. I heard an elder once remark, "If you don't know where you are going, any road will get you there." This modest insight may sum up better than any National Indian Education reports, panels, or committees the crisis of not just Indian education today, but education in America.

Today what counts as knowledge in mainstream education is too often short-term memorization of "facts." What counts as understanding is specialization in a narrow topic within a field or discipline. Understanding is so narrowly framed that it is often difficult for the specialists, let alone students, to effectively connect or relate their knowledge and understanding to the everyday lives of nonscientists. Because people desire just the "facts" without any understanding of the relations and connections between the "facts" and the rest of the world, we have the search-engine model of education. Faster, more powerful, and increasingly smaller computers, though great at processing data and performing quantitative analysis, cannot tell us what the data mean.

We are drowning in information, the bits and pieces of dot.com minutiae that more often than not are advertisements and amusements; swimming in knowledge (the organized insights into highly specialized aspects of the phenomenal world—significant parts of our experience), albeit at various depths; and dying of thirst for what Deloria calls understanding and I would call wisdom, a "big picture," a worldview in which information and knowledge are integrated meaningfully. Deloria's discussion of American Indian notions of knowledge and understanding reminds us that ultimately, understanding or wisdom ought to be the goal of education.

Lest this point be misunderstood, computers, the World Wide Web, and technology are not necessarily the problem. All of the above are quite simply tools—material and technological aspects of modern industrial societies. However, unlike prior technological innovations in human history, whose applications and implications seemed relatively obvious within specific environments (e.g., the bow, the block and tackle, the saddle and stirrup, etc.), information technology today seems little understood in terms of environmental and cultural contexts. Although one might think information technology, especially in light of its service toward what is often referred to as globalization, cannot possibly serve indigenous peoples and their places. However, the Global Learning and Observations to Benefit the Environment Project, an experiential and inquiry-based educational use of the World Wide Web, suggests there might be reason for some optimism. Imagine indigenous schoolchildren from Malaysia, the Altai mountains of Siberia, and the desert Southwest going out in their homelands and experientially learning about their environments, collecting their own "data," and learning how to analyze their data by doing, as opposed to being taught about, science. More importantly, the Internet and World Wide Web may in fact give indigenous peoples around the world the opportunity to compare notes on what is happening in their homelands and, even more significantly, discuss what their observations mean.

The heart of the problems facing Indian education in America is found in the largely abstract metaphysics of time, space, and energy. Western metaphysics yields a very different conception of reality than an experiential American Indian metaphysics of place and power. One crucial difference in the two metaphysics is that the Western concepts presume to objectively describe the world at the expense of taking for granted, or at least leaving undeveloped, issues and questions regarding the nature of reality—that is, what Deloria calls the personality of the human beings doing the conceptualizing. It is the philosophical equivalent of a radar scan for which the subject, the conceptualizer and intellectual model-builder, is off the screen and not even registering as a blip.

It is symptomatic of the problems of modern Western thought, and specifically science, that one has to look back to Socrates, over two millennia before Immanuel Kant, G.F.W. Hegel, Ralph Waldo Emerson, William James, and John Dewey place the problem of human consciousness and spirit back into the debate between idealist and realist metaphysics. Only when modern Western psychology, social psychology, and sociology are born is the problem of personhood or the subject picked up on the metaphysical radar of Western science. This fact alone is very symbolic of the major weakness of the Western metaphysics of time, space, and energy. The Western metaphysics of science makes identification of things and some basic interactions relatively easy to identify; however, it provides almost no "enlightenment" regarding living relationships, processes between subjects, and the formation of what Deloria calls personalities—be they plants, animals, or geologic and geographic features of the world where we reside.

Deloria's proposal that we explore an indigenous (in this case American Indian) metaphysics must be among the first projects American Indian educators undertake if we are to not only decolonize, but also actively "indigenize" and truly make Native educational institutions our own. American Indians have a long history of rejecting abstract theologies and metaphysical systems in place of experiential systems properly called indigenous—indigenous in the sense that people historically and culturally connected to places can and do draw on power located in those places. Stated simply, *indigenous* means "to be of a place." The oratories of Tecumseh, Ten Bears, Sitting Bull, and Chief Joseph, to name but a few great leaders, speak eloquently to this point.

Indigenous people represent a culture emergent from a place, and they actively draw on the power of that place physically and spiritually. Indigenism, as discussed here, is a body of thought advocating and elaborating diverse cultures in their broadest sense—for example, behavior, beliefs, values, symbols, and material products—emergent from diverse places. To indigenize an action or object is the act of making something of a place. The active process of making culture in its broadest sense of a place is called indigenization.

Cajete's work *Look to the Mountain* should be required reading for all teachers wanting to indigenize their pedagogy and curriculum and provide a framework for students to explore meaning in their life experiences. Western scientists and engineers are good at identifying the pieces, parts, and things in the world. This is commonly what we refer to as knowledge, "a set of technical beliefs [and, I would add, skills] which, upon mastering, admit the pupil to the social and economic structures of the larger society." Jacques Ellul's observation of nearly four decades ago in *The Technological Society*, that even the modern way of thinking has become technical or technology-shaped, today seems prescient.

Institutions of the larger society provide little support for the emotional and spiritual development of individuals. Tocqueville remarked in the 1830s that he was amazed that a society so deeply committed to diversity of opinion and free thought had so little of either. He also identified the real danger in American democracy as the tendency for Americans to become so preoccupied with their individual economic gain that little time remained for direct participation in public life or community. He seems to have been on target, for in American education the purpose seems less and less about shaping responsible and respectful persons and more about, as Deloria says, the "training of professionals."

The absence in formal education today of the discussion of meaning—or awareness of the emergence of meaning—in our lives shows the success of a metaphysics that uncritically and for the most part unconsciously shapes education for all Americans. And, as Deloria points out, science will leave the questions of meaning to those institutions that appear to scientists as the embodiment of fuzzy or unclear thinking: the discipline of psychology and/or the social institution of religion. Understood in the context of Western metaphysics as portrayed by Deloria, it is easy to understand the necessary separation in modern Western thought between science, and religion and psychology (in all but its most reductionist biochemical versions).

The deep opposition in Western thought between science and religion is the most critical and fundamental obstacle to integrating modern science and American Indian wisdom born of an experiential metaphysics. Our ancient Native understanding begins with the necessary task—the problematic—of establishing what Deloria calls our personality: who we are. Learning comes early in indigenous institutions, not through lectures but through experience: customs, habits, and practices. The primary lesson learned is and was that knowledge and understanding come from our relatives, the other "persons" or "beings" we have relationships with and depend on in order to live. And it is through these relationships, physical and psychological, indeed spiritual, that human beings begin to understand who, why, and even to some degree what we are. A value-free, neutral, objective science of things cannot give us that, and it is this discovery of meaning through very complex relationships that is the hallmark of American Indian education.

Given Western metaphysical systems, as Deloria has described them, it is fitting and predictable that many learned persons in Western civilization today are concerned about finding a solution to the energy crisis they created. Make no mistake about it, technology alone is neither the problem nor the solution. The real issue is how we live in modern industrial societies. Yet it is obvious that the citizens of modern industrial and/or postindustrial societies are lacking the wherewithal to solve the problem.

The problem is *not* finding, renewing, conserving, or producing more energy, and the solution is not another cutting-edge technology. From the standpoint of an American Indian metaphysics of place and power, the problem is not about something called energy, but more realistically about power and the places we live—basically, how we live. We should not underestimate the deep-seated roots of the problem. Where do we start? At the beginning. This was the approach Deloria took nearly four decades ago with the publication of *God Is Red,* and, I believe, remains the best approach. We need a generation or two of articulate American Indian philosophers, scientists, and engineers learning rather than being taught lessons our elders can demonstrate for us—right where they live.

I believe science is moving from a mechanistic reductionist model to a holistic nonlinear or complexity, model, science view. Consequently, it seems reasonable to speak of a convergence of new scientific theories and understanding with what I would call indigenous North American worldviews and intellectual traditions. The hypothesis I challenge scientists, engineers, historians of science, and ethnographers to explore is the extent to which much of the so-called new knowledge and understanding of complexity, nonlinear systems, and emergence resides in American Indian tribal customs, habits, and social organization: the way we lived and live. Here the use of a concept of habitude seems worth consideration. Although *A Dictionary of Modern English Usage* may see the word *habitude* as superfluous and synonymous with *habit,* I believe its use justified when considered as an attitude or awareness of a deep system of experiential relations on which the world is building or living. The key here is recognizing that experience is the undeveloped and untheorized site where the divisions between subjective and objective, material and spiritual, and an entire series of dichotomies disappear.

To many of us who are part of tribes with clan systems, an obvious example of what I mean by *habitude* is the understanding one acquired as a part of a clan-based social system: knowledge first and later an understanding that the clan system not only indicated a certain tribal human organization, but also actually existed as a symbolic representation of the ecology and environment that we human beings were and are a part of. Learning through custom and habit, a tribe's clan structures and societal roles and responsibilities conveyed a significant amount of knowledge. It is not only possible to figuratively lay out the clans of various tribes—for example, the plants, animals, features of the natural world, and material objects represented in clan names, totems, and interclan relations—and actually produce a report about where and how people lived, it is necessary to do so in order to understand the comprehensive nature of their geographic and ecological knowledge.

A good example from the southeastern United States would be a comparison of the Cherokee clan system to the Euchee clan system. The Euchee share a large number of clans with the Seminole, but we both have a clan that the mountainous Cherokee do not possess. Knowledge of where the Seminole and Euchee historically resided solves the puzzle. The Seminole, living in the rich wetlands of south and central Florida, and the Euchee, who settled along the shores of the Savannah River but hunted throughout the Southeast and into northern Florida, have alligator clans, and the Cherokee do not. Considering where both tribes lived it is clear why the Seminole and Euchee acknowledge an important relationship with an animal species that the Cherokee do not.

Looking at the interfaces between our indigenous customs, habits, and ceremonies and our identity, spiritual being, and the natural world, it is clear that a rich repository of knowledge exists that suburban commuters cannot download from the internet. The general public has so divorced their lives from places, environments, and living ecosystems that it is easy to understand the ignorant questions often asked about American Indians—for example, "What is the American Indian religion?" Well, for whom, which American Indians, where? Yes, the Euchee lived on a river, but we did not have a Salmon Ceremony; Native people of the eastern Chesapeake Bay region never had Buffalo Ceremonies.

It is obvious when we consider the symbolic aspects of our cultures, ceremonial life, and even the social organization—the clan systems and special societies we created in our tribal communities—that these all contained accurate empirical information about how our ancestors lived in relationships with real ecosystems and environments.

In fact, I would suggest that there is knowledge contained in these cultural practices that modern science cannot acquire using a mechanistic and dissective approach, especially when the Western idea of universal objective truth reduces itself to abstract mathematical formulas. Western science is very good at that. But contrast this knowledge system and its product to one where knowledge claims literally emerge from a place—an experience in the world. This kind of knowledge will be fundamentally different from the knowledge produced through laboratory experiment or dissection.

You see and hear things by being in a forest, on a river, or at an ocean coastline; you gain real experiential knowledge that you cannot see by looking at the beings that live in those environments under a microscope or in a laboratory experiment. You experience places and learn, if attentive about processes and relationships in those places.

When we start examining issues of complexity, emergence, the principles of self-organization, the biological phenomena of morphological or structural change within species, all of that knowledge is perfectly and completely consistent with indigenous worldviews. Our ancestors understood that the world is a dynamic and living place. I am not aware of any Native traditions that do not as a part of their oral histories accept that changes have occurred over time, often in a very short time sequence, catastrophic and otherwise. Some are more formal about this than others—Hopi and Diné traditions have very explicit discussions about the different stages of creation that have occurred. The fundamental notion is that the world and its entire biosphere is a dynamic living system.

This insight of course leads to the recognition that traditional ecological knowledge culture (e.g., language, tools, clothing, technology, etc.) in nonindustrial or nonmodern societies is emergent from specific places of the planet. Throughout Africa, Asia, the Pan-Pacific Rim, and to the homelands of our brothers and sisters in Central and South America, traditional Native peoples possess personalities and culture born of places. The power we possess as Potawatomi, Ute, Abanaki, Salish, Lummi—as indigenous peoples—is found in places even today. The power we still possess, although it is constantly threatened and in many peoples greatly impoverished, expresses itself in an attitude of humility and moral integrity still found most often in our elders. Not only wisdom sits in places, as Keith Basso reminds us in his work on the Western Apache, but so does power and personality.

This realization offers a powerful way of talking about the manner in which biological diversity and cultural diversity are intimately connected. It requires recognition that culture is an emergent property—that is, a reality resulting from a complex process containing a multitude of interactions. In short, cultures have causes, but not the kind most biologists or social scientists can easily test in a laboratory or replicate in linear causal models. Because the world we inhabit is a very diverse place, we ought to understand what nearly all American Indian worldviews readily acknowledge: cultural diversity is not an issue of political correctness but is a geographic, historical, and biological reality.

Recognizing this point highlights the most devastating feature of the Western worldview in its general character and practical application: the destructive notion already forming by the time Cristobal Colon (Columbus) arrived in the Caribbean Islands that Europeans possessed the Truth and that it was their job to make sure all people they met on the planet were shown the Truth. This confidence, initially buttressed by the domination of the Church, that Western civilization represented the highest development of humankind was central to the Western worldview. The mandate to do things the way they did, pray the way they did, and virtually live the way they did was and, sadly, remains symptomatic of the extent to which the Western worldview of learned Europeans was already an abstract time-based ideology. They literally could not understand any history other than their own because their history became and was understood as The World History.

If one understands this Western self-conscious faith in (1) abstract universal truths and (2) the European moral duty to remake the world (in accordance with these truths) in their own image, then the incredible force of these ideas explains much of human history for the last 500 years. The worldview shaped by this twofold faith precluded recognition of knowledge, understanding, and power residing in places. It informs the practices of colonialism yesterday and today, and it suggests just how important cultural diversity is to the life of the planet and its people.

Before Hegel, the preeminent modern idealist, developed his idea of world spirit, Kant had written two telling essays: "Idea of a Universal History with a Cosmopolitan Intent" and "What Is Enlightenment?" Both essays signal very clearly the profoundly interior nature of the world Kant lived in and the extent to which reason (i.e., rationality), history, progress, and enlightenment itself were understood as embodied in the world and reflected in the modern Western worldview. The manifestation of European Enlightenment idealism in the institutions of Western Europe had a very dark side, one that Nietzsche, Dewey, Marx, and the Frankfort School of critical theorists all saw in one respect or another, but that indigenous peoples all over the world experienced.

Again it matters little if you were (are) in Asia, Africa, South America, or Malaysia. The treatment of Native peoples around the world is an ex post facto demonstration of the Western linear idea of history, where Western Europeans understood themselves to be at the cutting-edge of history with everybody else requiring instruction to be brought "up to speed." This idea, so informative of European colonialism, was and is pure ideology, and if turnabout is fair play, the best example of what we Indians would call modern Western "mythology."

Western European colonizers were not tolerant of people who refused their instruction. This is a still living history—it is not a contentious claim. By the time of the American and French Revolutions, those few Europeans receiving a formal education had been taught that their way of living signaled the highest development of human potential as could exist in this world. While such talk has ended in this age of political correctness, the walk has not. Western-inspired institutions continue to walk (behave) the old Western way. Just ask indigenous peoples throughout the world, who are often fighting to keep from being trampled over.

It is not enough to simply collect oral histories, study the language, learn the toolmaking procedures, and know the arts and crafts of our indigenous societies. All of this is being done and ought to be done, but we must explore experientially living in the world. Unless we incorporate features of our cultures into a holistic and integrated indigenous process of education, what we have produced is most likely "educational tokenism."

What we still possess, amazingly, not as individuals but as members of tribes, not nation-states, is big-picture wisdom born of experience, not pedagogical indoctrination. The work ahead of us is at once exciting and daunting. The task is daunting, for to a great extent we must undertake something our ancestors never had the necessity, opportunity, or wherewithal to undertake: an explicit discussion about the metaphysical foundation underlying our diverse indigenous worldviews. The work is exciting because it plays to our strengths: customs, habits, values, and how we live as indigenous people, not in some romanticized ideal or abstract past, but in the world. Power and place equal personality: Deloria's formulation is founded on experience in the world. A good place to begin Indian education in America is with the lived experiences of peoples who have resided in places long enough to know and remember what it means to be Native to a place.

# KNOWING AND
# UNDERSTANDING

*V. Deloria*

Modern American education is a major domestic industry. With the collapse of the cold war, education may well become the industry of the American future. Indeed, in the 2000 election both candidates stressed education. Because education significantly impacts Indian communities and has exerted great influence among Indians from the very beginning of European contact, it is our duty to draw back from the incessant efforts to program educational opportunities, and evaluate what we are doing and where we are going in this field. It should come as no surprise to people in Indian communities that in recent months one report on Indian community colleges has been released, and plans have been announced to conduct yet another study on what is happening in Indian education. We seem to occupy the curious position of being pilot projects and experimental subjects for one group of educators, and the last communities to receive educational benefits as determined by another set of educators, primarily administrators. So the time has come to try to make sense of what education has been, presently is, and conceivably might be for American Indians.

The Western scientist has been personified, by Western peoples themselves, as Dr. Faustus, Dr. Frankenstein, and Dr. Strangelove—the person who steps outside the boundary of acceptable behavior and becomes a monster and a threat to humankind. One of the pressing ethical questions of today, with regard to genetics and atomic research, is whether when we think we can do something, we are then obligated to do it. The real question should be whether what we propose is ethical in the larger sense, not whether or not we can do something. This missing element of the ethical is a value that can only be properly understood in the Indian context.

European civilization has a determined and continuing desire to spread its view of the world to non-European countries. Within a generation of the conquest of Mexico, the Spanish had founded schools in Mexico City for the education of indigenous youths. An important part of mission activities for the next 300 years was the education of both young people and adults in the Christian religion and the niceties of European customs. French colonial policy dictated a kind of education in which prominent families within the Indian tribe and the French colonial families exchanged children for a short period of time. This was to ensure that customs would be properly understood and civility between the two groups would not be violated by thoughtless or ignorant actions.

English education, represented first by benevolent members of the aristocracy who gave funds to support Indian schools, and later embodied in the U.S. government's encouragement of mission activities among the frontier tribes, represented, and still represents, an effort to effect a complete transformation of beliefs and behaviors of Indians. Education in the English-American context resembles indoctrination more than it does other forms of teaching because it insists on implanting a particular body of knowledge and a specific view of the world, which often does not correspond to the life experiences that people have or might be expected to encounter. With some modifications, and with a considerable reduction in the intensity of educational discipline, the education that Indians receive today is the highly distilled product of Christian/European scientific and political encounters with the world and is undergirded by specific but generally unarticulated principles of interpretation. Because the product is so refined and concise, education has become something different and apart from the lives of people and is seen as a set of technical beliefs, which, upon mastering, admit the pupil to the social and economic structures of the larger society. Nowhere is this process more evident than in science and engineering, fields in which an increasing number of American Indian students are now studying.

Education today trains professionals but it does not produce people. It is, indeed, not expected to produce personality growth, in spite of elaborate and poetic claims made by some educators. We need only look at the conflict, confusion, and controversy over prayer in schools, sex education, and the study of non-Western societies and civilizations to see that the goal of modern education is to produce people trained to function within an institutional setting as a contributing part of a vast socioeconomic machine. The dissolution of the field of ethics into a bewildering set of subfields of professional ethics further suggests that questions of personality and personal values must wait until the individual has achieved some measure of professional standing.

This condition, the separation of knowledge into professional expertise and personal growth, is an insurmountable barrier for many Indian students. It creates severe emotional problems as the students seek to sort out the proper principles from these two isolated parts of human experience. The problem arises because in traditional Indian society there is no separation; there is, in fact, a reversal of the sequencer in which non-Indian education occurs: in traditional society the goal is to ensure personal growth and then to develop professional expertise. Even the most severely eroded Indian community today still has a substantial fragment of the old ways left, and these ways are to be found in the Indian family. Even the badly shattered families preserve enough elements of kinship so that whatever the experiences of the young, there is a sense that life has some unifying principles that can be discerned through experience and that guide behavior. This feeling, and it is a strong emotional feeling toward the world that transcends beliefs and information, continues to gnaw at American Indians throughout their lives.

It is singularly instructive to move away from Western educational values and theories and survey the educational practices of the old Indians. Not only does one get a sense of emotional stability, which indeed might be simply the impact of nostalgia, but viewing the way the old people educated themselves and their young gives a person a sense that education is more than the process of imparting and receiving information. Indeed, that it is the very purpose of human society, and human societies cannot really flower until they understand the parameters of possibilities that the human personality contains.

The old ways of educating affirmed the basic principle that human personality was derived from accepting the responsibility to be a contributing member of a society. Kinship and clan were built upon the idea that individuals owed each other certain kinds of behaviors, and that if each individual performed his or her task properly, society as a whole would function. Because everyone was related to everyone else in some specific manner, by giving to others within the society, a person was enabled to receive what was necessary to survive and prosper. The worst punishment, of course, was banishment, as it meant that the individual had been placed beyond the boundaries of organized life.

The family was not, however, the nuclear family of modern-day America, nor was it even the modern Indian family, which has, in addition to its blood-related members, an FBI undercover agent, an anthropologist, a movie maker, and a white psychologist looking for a spiritual experience. The family was rather a multigenerational complex of people, and clan and kinship responsibilities extended beyond the grave and far into the future. Remembering a distant ancestor's name and achievements might be equally as important as feeding a visiting cousin or showing a niece how to sew and cook. Children were greatly beloved by most tribes, and this feeling gave evidence that the future was as important as the present or past, a fact that policy makers and treaty signers have deliberately chosen to ignore as part of the Indian perspective on life.

Little emphasized, but equally important for the formation of personality, was the group of other forms of life that had come down over the centuries as part of the larger family. Neoshamanism today pretends that one need only go into a sweat lodge or trance and find a "power animal." Many people, Indians and non-Indians, are consequently wandering around today with images of power panthers in the backs of their minds. But there seems to have been a series of very early covenants between certain human families and specific birds, fish, grazing animals, predatory animals, and reptiles. One need only view the several generations of Indian families with some precision to understand that very specific animals will appear in vision quests, sweat lodges, trances, and psychic experiences over and over again. For some reason these animals are connected to the families over a prolonged period of time and offer their assistance and guidance during times of crisis during each generation of humans.

Birds, animals, plants, and reptiles do not appear as isolated individuals anymore than humans appear in that guise. Consequently, the appearance of one animal suggests that the related set of other forms of life is nearby, is willing to provide assistance, and a particular role to play in the growth of human personality. In the traditional format there is no such thing as isolation from the rest of creation, and the fact of this relatedness provides a basic context within which education in the growth of personality and the acquisition of technical skills can occur. There is, of course, a different set of other forms of life for each human family, and so dominance and worthlessness do not form the boundaries between the human species and other forms of life.

Education in the traditional setting occurs by example and not as a process of indoctrination. That is to say, elders are the best living examples of what the end product of education and life experiences should be. We sometimes forget that life is exceedingly hard and that none of us accomplishes everything we could possibly do, or even many of the things we intended to do. The elder exemplifies both the good and the bad experiences of life, and in witnessing their failures as much as their successes we are cushioned in our despair of disappointment and bolstered in our exuberance of success. But a distinction should be made here between tribal and nontribal peoples. For some obscure reason, nontribal peoples tend to judge their heroes much more harshly than do tribal peoples. Tribal peoples expect a life of perfection and thereby partially deify their elders. At least they once did. Today, watching the ethical failures of the non-Indian politician, sports hero, and television preacher, it is not difficult to conclude that nontribal peoples have no sense of morality and integrity at all.

The final ingredient of traditional tribal education is that accomplishments are regarded as the accomplishments of the family and are not attributed to the world around us. We share our failures and successes so that we know who we are and so that we have confidence when we do things. Traditional knowledge enables us to see our place and our responsibility within the movement of history as it is experienced by the community. Formal American education, on the other hand, helps us to understand how things work, and knowing how things work and being able to make them work are the marks of a professional person in this society. It is critically important that we do not confuse these two kinds of knowledge or exchange the roles they play in our lives. The major shortcoming in American institutional life is that most people cannot distinguish these two ways of knowing; and for many Americans there is no personal sense of knowing who they are, so professionalism always overrules the concern for persons.

Today we see a great revival of traditional practices in many tribes. Younger people are bringing back crafts, songs and dances, and religious ceremonies to make them the center of their lives. These restorations are important symbols of a sense of community, but they must be accompanied by hard and clear thinking that can distinguish what is valuable in the old ways from the behavior we are expected to practice as members of the larger American society. In this movement it is very important for younger Indians to take the lead in restoring the sense of family, clan, and community responsibility that undergird the traditional practices. In doing so, the next generation of Indians will be able to bring order and stability to Indian communities, not because of their professional expertise but because of their personal examples.

# THE SCHIZOPHRENIC
# NATURE OF
# WESTERN METAPHYSICS

*D. Wildcat*

In order to clearly "distinguish what is valuable in the old ways from the behavior we are expected to practice as members of the larger American society," American Indians must elaborate our own indigenous systems of metaphysics and contrast them with the dominant metaphysics of Western civilization. Failure to deal with the problem of practices and values at their roots or foundations will result in serious confusion later.

The best way to illustrate the fundamental difference between a Western metaphysics and an indigenous North American metaphysics is to begin with the most vexing issue confronting Western-influenced societies: the irreconcilable duality between facts and values, most often discussed as the science-versus-religion conflict. We are flooded with media reports of the conflicts daily—for example, the evolution controversy, human cloning, abortion, development of biological and nuclear weaponry, use of animals in medical research, product safety testing, and so on. What is the source of these conflicts?

EXPERIENTIAL METAPHYSICS IN THE WORLD

An American Indian response, I would argue, would identify the source of many of these conflicts in the failure of Western metaphysics to produce an integrated big picture of human experience in the world as opposed to a big picture of the world. The distinction between an indigenous metaphysics of human beings in the world versus a Western metaphysics of the world is crucial. The latter requires a level of abstraction beyond human experience, while the former requires abstract concept formation in the service of experience.

The "metaphysics of the world" is nothing less than the transference and unconscious resurrection of the medieval "God problem" as the modern Western problem of the certainty of human knowledge. Medieval scholastic philosophers successfully demonstrated through logic that God must be omnipresent, omniscient, and omnipotent. In the seventeenth and eighteenth centuries logic was of little use in addressing growing doubt among Western intellectuals of the existence of God, although logic was increasingly demonstrated as useful to humans in their attempts to control and use nature. Today the irreconcilable conflict between meaning/values and knowledge/facts in Western metaphysics is obvious. This is clearly demonstrated in the inability of Western legal institutions to grasp American Indian and Alaska Native claims that some places on the planet possess a degree of sacredness that precludes treatment as real estate, private property, or public lands. Nowhere is the schizophrenic nature of Western metaphysics more obvious than in the current lack of religious freedom for many indigenous people in America.

The poverty of religious freedom is evidenced in recent U.S. Supreme Court decisions that increasingly reduce religion to a set of deeply held beliefs unrelated to where people live and how they live. At the very moment people around the world are awakened to the fact that our planet is one complex web of ecological systems resplendent with biological and cultural diversity, the group of people most representative of cultural and ethnic diversity in the United States—American Indians and Alaska Natives—are implored to explain their widely shared understanding that the earth is sacred. It is ironic that the most diverse peoples of the Americas are now placed in a position where we are required to explain, document, and provide evidence for our spiritual and religious traditions in order to protect religious ceremonies and practices that ensure the very biological diversity that our spiritual traditions rest on.

This turn of events is not surprising given the dominant Western view that religion is not of this world—in other words, natural but an other-worldly (supernatural) phenomenon. Since long before the passage of the American Indian Religious Freedom Act in 1978, American Indians and Alaska Natives have been fighting to defend the notion—no, the practical reality—that religious experiences are in a profound sense a part of the power that "sits in places." We reject abstract theologies and metaphysical systems in the place of experiential systems properly called indigenous or emergent from a place.

What explains the tremendous divide between our experiential traditions and Western theological abstractions? Two very different metaphysical systems: Native systems, where explanation is often discussed in terms of experiential correspondence and understood as irreducible to simple mechanical causality, versus the now dominant Western metaphysical system, where the logic of causality established by David Hume nearly three centuries ago mandates empirical generalizations of mechanical cause-and-effect relationships.

## The Problem with Descartes and Hume

The conflict between science and religion in the Western tradition is indicative of the schizophrenic nature of Western metaphysics. An American Indian metaphysics has the advantage of designating science and religion not as mutually exclusive realms of experience or areas of human interest, but as fundamental questions of knowledge and understanding found on a "continuum of experience." It is not an overstatement to see Descartes's deductive, even mathematical, rationalism and Hume's systematic empiricism as flip sides of the same coin. Both point to a world encountered by learned European minds as being without spirit or power in a tangible phenomenal sense. Although Descartes's rationalism seems to emphasize the human mind or, as one modern philosopher remarked, place a "ghost in the machine," this does not discount the basic point that his clear and distinct ideas are only appertained within a human mind that is understood as a logical machine.

Teaching American Indian and Alaska Native students Descartes's *Meditations on First Philosophy* and *Discourse on Method of Rightly Conducting Reason and Reaching the Truth in the Sciences* is difficult because the problem he poses is foreign to the general metaphysical foundation of indigenous North American worldviews. To doubt one's own existence seems not only unreasonable but suggestive of serious illness within indigenous worldviews. The famous "I think, therefore I am" is an ex post facto truism not only at the level of logic but at the level of experience too. That Descartes found it necessary to logically prove something that could be accepted by virtue of experience only indicates the extent to which experience in the world became increasingly problematic for the Western psyche.

Descartes's focus on subject-centered, self-conscious awareness is interesting and peculiar. Subjective awareness and consciousness would seem a good bridge to an exploration of human experience in a broader context. However, what I will call Descartes's extreme logical interiorizing of awareness in his "I think, therefore I am" precludes any such exploration. Existence in a Cartesian worldview is so intellectually abstract relative to experience that we might suggest Descartes initiates a modern tradition of experiential agnosticism—that is, experience as unknowable—in Western thought. What may be even more amazing and ironic is that Hume's radically empiricist version of human experience and existence produces a similar agnostic view of experience, albeit from a completely opposite point of departure.

Hume's response to the increasingly problematic nature of experience in the world was set out in *A Treatise of Human Nature*, and later in a reworking of part one of that work known as *An Enquiry Concerning Human Understanding*. Hume's notion that ultimately all knowledge comes from sense impressions results in his claim that causality is nothing more than a constant combination between perceived objects called causes and effects. In fact, he consistently and quite radically claims that any so-called natural laws of causality are little more than empirical generalizations based on custom and habit. He denies there exists any necessary relation or connection between objects. Not surprisingly, Native students often remark that after Hume's inquiry all that remains for certain are uncertain beliefs and no knowledge.

Hume's *Enquiry* is rightly recognized as the benchmark for modern skepticism, but from the standpoint of an American Indian metaphysics, Hume's thought is fatally flawed by the reduction of experience to impressions of objects and their more vague relations. Not surprisingly, Hume's attitude toward God and miracles is skepticism, as both by definition within Hume's philosophical epistemology (system of knowledge) are outside the realm of knowledge—irreducible to impressions. If one reduces experience to impressions of objects, then much of what challenges our understanding in the world will be unintelligible. Hume demonstrated that empiricism and rationalism both result in reasoned skepticism, but to what end? The obvious point is that Hume's "miracles" confront him as nothing more than mysteries or events without explanation at the present time or beyond reason. It would indeed be an improvement if scientists today read and understood Hume, for at least some modesty regarding their own knowledge claims would certainly ensue.

Unfortunately, the part of Hume's thought that was most lasting was his simple construction of cause and effect and the reduction of all causal relationships to the constant conjunction of objects. These two ideas have certainly served the mechanics-illustrated view of life well.

The problem with seventeenth- and eighteenth-century rationalism and empiricism is that both left undeveloped (or one might even say avoided) the realm of experience and, consequently, the realm of power. An alternative to Hume's empiricism (and inevitable skepticism) and Descartes's rationalism is a reconstruction of American Indian metaphysics suggested by Deloria: a reconstruction that overcomes the Western dualisms of knowledge versus beliefs, and science versus religion. The difficult task for many of us first-generation "academic" intellectuals —Euchee, Lakota, Salish, or otherwise—is to recognize that the wisdom we want to explore is born of experience. In addition, for those *traditional* scholars or elders deeply imbued with this understanding, self-conscious discussion or analysis of their so-called metaphysical systems would be difficult at best and may rightly seem foolish or dangerous—possibly both.

Fortunately, we academically trained Native scholars have an advantage. If we avoid the traps of Western metaphysical schizophrenia, we can explore indigenous systems of thought by becoming attentive to how our traditional scholars or elders continue to live. The incredible gulf between Western and indigenous metaphysics is best summed up as follows: in the Western context metaphysics became a study for philosophers; in indigenous communities metaphysics would be understood as the basis for living well—attentively, respectfully, and responsibly—in this world.

RELIGIOUS BELIEFS VERSUS
SCIENTIFIC KNOWLEDGE

As we enter the twenty-first century, the fact that Native students are often confused by the question "What is the difference between knowledge and beliefs?" is hopeful. For unlike many non-Indian students today who think their beliefs, as such, excuse them from having any intelligible discussion in support of these beliefs or correspondence with reality, American Indians and Alaska Natives still seem to grasp that beliefs are most fundamentally about what we know and understand.

A very good friend and scholar in the Western tradition, George Kaull, used to constantly say, "Faith is believing something you know ain't so," and, "Religion is the problem!" As a student of the Western tradition, I understood his point: for if knowledge becomes reducible to materialist mechanics, and those experiences and most deeply felt aspects of our existence are irreducible to such mechanical explanations, then religion (broadly understood as encompassing such aspects and experiences of our existence) becomes a realm of faith: unknowable and unexplainable.

Indigenous American Indian religions exist independent of this metaphysical burden. While explainability seems necessary in rationalist accounts of religion, it makes religion merely a large set of potentially infinite, abstract logical systems. So what one begins to know about religion in the Western tradition is a philosophical system or theology. Faith becomes critical and necessary when one wants to know how these elaborate abstract systems correspond or operate in the world, for there exists within the dominant Western metaphysics no way of knowing—in other words, Descartes's doubt or Hume's skepticism.

American Indian, essentially tribal, religious traditions offer a stark contrast to the metaphysical schizophrenia submerged deep in the Western tradition. First, rationalist explanation is unnecessary if one depends on experience. This does not make the discussion of religion easy, it merely suggests that what we can discuss is limited, not just by tribal tradition, but by its very nature (reality). Indigenous people might agree with Hume, although for much different reasons, that the most meaningful aspects of religion are unexplainable by either the rationalist or the empiricist mandates of Western metaphysics. However, in the continuum of experience, indigenous people depend on experiential verification, not logical proof.

It is not the least bit personally or communally troubling to indigenous peoples that all of our human experiences, especially "religious" experiences, are not reducible to objects or logic. William James's *The Varieties of Religious Experience* debunked what he called "medical materialism" over a century ago, and his basic critique of scientific explanations of religious experiences still holds up. Experience remains the unexplored metaphysical terrain of the twenty-first century. And it is likely that the best scouts will be Indians—not by virtue of superior "intellect" as commonly understood, but simply because there remains among many of us a predisposition to live in the world as opposed to living on, above, or in control of the world.

Sam Deloria gave an excellent illustration of the fundamental difference in Western and indigenous worldviews during a presentation at Haskell Indian Nations University. He commented that one of the difficulties in having our traditional elders testify before

Congress on issues relating to "religion" or "religious freedom" was the immediate miscommunication that ensued. When asked by committee members to speak about their religion, elders would often respond by telling committee members that they did not have a "religion." They were absolutely right, but their stance was predictably confusing to congressional committee members, who were in no position to understand what our traditional scholars and spiritual leaders were telling them.

Osage theologian George Tinker summarizes the basis for this communication problem quite well:

> Most adherents of traditional American Indian ways characteristi-
> cally deny that their people ever engaged in any religion at all.
> Rather, these spokespeople insist, their whole culture and social
> structure was and still is infused with a spirituality that cannot be
> separated from the rest of the community's life at any point.
> Whereas outsiders may identify a single ritual as the "religion" of a
> particular people, the people themselves will likely see that cere-
> mony as merely an extension of their day-to-day existence, all parts
> of which are expressed within ceremonial parameters and shall be
> seen as "religious."

The sacredness of life was felt, acknowledged, and expressed throughout one's activities in the world.

It is difficult to say exactly why experience in the world became so frightful to civilized Western humankind. *God Is Red* made a good case: the problems ensued shortly after the life of Jesus was no longer seen as the life of a single community member in a very specific place on the planet, but as the outline for an abstract, worldwide, theology-based religion. But other events seem to have played a role too, including rapid technological advancement, development of the modern nation-state (or reemergence there-of), and incredible social and biological catastrophe in the fif-teenth century. It seems plausible that Kirkpatrick Sale's judgment in *The Conquest of Paradise* of the voyages of Cristobal Colon may be right: Columbus was not so much trying to discover a new land but escape a declining, chaos-ridden old land.

The distrust of experience is nowhere more evident, as we have seen, than in the philosophy of Descartes, who logically introduces God as a kind of insurance policy for reality. And the fear of experience in the world may have been the motive for the greatly diminished conception of experience in Locke's and Hume's empiricism. Nevertheless, Descartes's rationalism offers little hope of resolving the dual personality of Western metaphysics, as abstract logic affords establishment of as many gods as human beings can think up.

Humankind may indeed have a gift for thinking things up, creativity, imagination, and inventiveness, but human societies and the earth's ecosystems seem threatened by a human creativity and imagination that has literally and figuratively lost touch with the earth. My friend George Kaull came to believe late in life that science also had a share of the "problem" he used to ascribe to religion. If faith is "believing things you know ain't so," a good number of scientists are guilty.

The silence of the sciences about the most pressing problems of our world today is indicative of the schizophrenic nature of the metaphysics underlying much of their modern practices. Descartes's rationalism and Hume's empiricism are flip sides of the same coin, a worldview in which humans presume themselves to be the measure of all things. Unfortunately, neither tackles the real question—so what of humankind, what of this unit of measure, so to speak?

The problem with Western science (both rationalist and empiricist denominations) reminds me of what the great pitcher Satchel Page told a young player seeking advice. To paraphrase: "Remember, it's not what you don't know that gets you in trouble, it's what you know that just ain't so that causes problems."

# TRADITIONAL
# TECHNOLOGY

*V. Deloria*

Education today is wholly oriented toward science and secularism. At the core of every curriculum is the belief that we can look at phenomena with a completely rational and objective eye and find abstract principles underlying all behavior, from atoms to masses of people. This perspective implies, of course, that the natural world and its inhabitants are completely materialistic, and that even the most profound sentiments can be understood as electrical impulses in the brain or as certain kinds of chemical reactions. We have arrived at this state of affairs through the application of a methodology of reductionism, a tendency to divide, subdivide, and subdivide again in order to find the constituents of an entity or event.

The reductionist view of the world is further enhanced by the spectacular success of modern technology. Natural forces are being brought under human control, and cosmic energies bring us both power and entertainment. If a person were to chart out the relationships of the various academic disciplines, the resulting outline might find physics and mathematics as coequal partners at the top of a pyramid of knowledge with chemistry, biology, psychology, and eventually the humanities as imperfect subsets or special cases of the application of physics to selected phenomena. This outline has dominated most of this century, but recent theoretical developments are now beginning to call this simplistic perspective to account. The Gaia Hypothesis, among other new theories, suggests that we should begin to look at things organically and that we might indeed be a minor episode in a larger scheme of life. Whether this hypothesis proves fruitful enough to

become a dominant paradigm in the social/scientific future is be-
side the point. The issue today is that we are no longer bound to
use mechanistic models exclusively to tell us how to think about
the world.

The knowledge and technology of tribal peoples, primitive
peoples, and ancient humans does not really appear in the modern
scientific scheme, unless it is to be found within the minor articu-
lations of the concept of cultural evolution hidden in the backwa-
ters of anthropology, sociology, and history. This knowledge that
served our ancestors so well emerges from time to time when
modern scientists advocate a novel interpretation of data and, in
order to claim some historical roots for their ideas—as new ideas
are forbidden in academia— ancient or tribal peoples are cited as
societies who once used certain practices or held certain beliefs.
But the presentation of the ideas is usually accompanied by the
patronizing view that although tribals and primitives did originate
the idea or the practice, they could not have possibly understood
its significance.

What would be some of the aspects of traditional technology?
Foremost would be establishing relationships with the larger cosmic rhythms and following those cycles. It is not simply correlat-
ing the growth of corn with the maturing of mountain plants as
earlier mentioned. The Tohono O'odham regulated their harvest
of desert plants according to the passage of star formations so that
other creatures could use the desert plants when it was best for
them, humans standing aside while they did so, after which humans
could harvest what they needed. Technology would be the burning
of woods and grasses to ensure proper growth and elimination of
the buildup of undergrowth that would cause catastrophic fires.
Traditional technology involved knowing when to harvest plants
and how to approach them. Sand cherries would be sour if picked
when the wind was blowing from humans to plants and sweet
when it blew from plants to humans.

Immense knowledge of horses was possessed by many tribes. An
old tradition says that the Nez Perce created the Appaloosa by putting mud compacts on pregnant mares where they wanted spots to

be on the colts when they were born. Bows made from different kinds of wood produced different effects, and consequently people had to wait until the different woods could be harvested for bows. Teas and poultices made from herbs had to be harvested at the right time or they would not have the proper potency. Watching birds approach and use trees and shrubs enabled people to learn the correct time for harvesting. Medicine rocks abounded and certain kinds of crystals were used for divining future events. Watching how animals related to each other often showed the best ways to approach various animals. Almost everything in nature gave lessons on how the human should most profitably live.

Indian students who come from traditional homes have considerable difficulty assimilating the practices and beliefs they learned as children with the modernist attitude of science. And for Indian students who grew up in urban areas and whose experience in reservation communities is limited to sporadic summertime visits, an even greater difficulty in assimilating this attitude exists. These students often believe certain things about tribal knowledge and techniques as a matter of faith because their experiences are very limited. But they want to recapture as much knowledge of their own tribal past and practices as possible, so the problem becomes an emotional as well as an intellectual dilemma.

A good deal of the traditional knowledge was placed in a family context so that it was not difficult to remember. Thus animals and plants were believed to be not simply peoples but families within that peoplehood. It was therefore possible to establish intimate relationships with specific plants and animals and gain the precise knowledge that they possessed about the world. Although much of that knowledge has been lost with the confinement of our peoples to small reservations, it is still possible for the next generation of Indians to regain much information that we once had. Through precise observation and through ceremonies, we can once again connect with the lives and minds of the other entities of the creation.

Today numerous new studies suggest that many species have their own languages. Birds, prairie dogs, beavers, bears, and others are now given credit for having a substantial mental and emotional life. One might even project that they have their philosophies as we have ours. It would be foolish to deny that possibility when purchasing tapes of whale songs at our local New Age store. Now, these creatures often spoke to our grandparents in our language and also taught them some of their language. Imitating birds and animals was not simply an entertainment talent but spoke of the intimacy of organic life in a way that Western science may take decades to understand. So at many points where the West relies on doctrinal explanations, traditional Indian knowledge can provide both ideas and data to bridge the gulf and expand human understanding.

CREATION STORIES

If one should track backward into the past of most tribal groups to find how things originated, one would quickly discover that specific instructions were given to the old people regarding plants, animals, birds and reptiles, and stones, as well as the technology for living in community with them. These instructions came in dreams, visions, and unusual incidents, and more often than not the relationship with plants and animals was a result of interspecies communications. The primary focus of creation stories of many tribes placed human beings as among the last creatures who were created and as the youngest of the living families. We were given the ability to do many things, but not specific wisdom about the world. So our job was to learn from other, older beings and to pattern ourselves after their behavior. We were to gather knowledge, not dispense it. Western science really traces itself backward to the Garden of Eden scenario in which humans are also last created, but it is believed that they are given mastery over the rest of the world. Humans are, in the Western scheme of things, the source of knowledge and information, but they are also isolated from the rest of creation by standing alone at the top of the pyramid.

Because we gather knowledge from older beings who have the wisdom of the world within their grasp, we must maintain a relationship with the rest of creation. Consequently, the clan and kinship systems that guided the social organization of the world were not only modeled after observed behavior of other beings, but also sought to preserve the idea of relationships of the natural world within the technology that arose as a result of our learning experiences. Western science learned its lessons from observation and then from experimentation with the entities of the natural world. There was no sense of community because humans had been placed too far above the rest of creation, and there was no hesitancy among Western people to use the rest of creation in any manner it could conceive. But the price of using others as objects was that absolute values had to be maintained, and space, time, and matter became absolute concepts within Western science. Both science and its reductionist methods remained absolute as long as these ideas were regarded as absolute.

In a fundamental sense, which many people in science do not yet recognize, the theories of Albert Einstein created tremendous gaps in the Western scientific scheme. Einstein's work challenged the absolute status of space, time, and matter, and his major contribution was to reduce the absolute nature of these ideas to a relative status; he introduced the context into modern science in a way that could not easily be refuted. But the importance of relativity for traditional thinking is that it began to shift the focus from the absolute materialistic framework science had constructed to an idea that things are related. Not many people in the academic community have yet applied this idea to the world as a totality, and certainly many of them would rebel at the idea that science is shifting significantly toward a tribal understanding of the world. They continue to believe that relativity means that there are no absolutes. In fact it means that things are related in some fundamental ways that had previously been excluded. There may not be as many anomalies and coincidences as we have previously supposed.

Many tribes described relationships in terms of correspondence between two things ordinarily thought to be distinct, isolated, or unrelated. The old saying in religious ceremonies, "as above so it is on earth," is such a correspondence; so is the gathering of things for equipping medicine bags, for making drums, weapons, household goods, and clothing, and for creating altars and blessing dwellings. In each of these activities a variety of materials are used, and they are said to "represent" certain things. *Represent* here is not taken as a symbolic gesture, but usually to mean that the power and knowledge of these things are actually present in the creation of something new.

## WISDOM AND VISION
### ACKNOWLEDGING THE LIFE AND POWER IN ALL THINGS

Today we have the artifacts of every tribe lining the shelves of museums and being described as great primitive art. And, indeed, if we think of these artifacts only as useful utensils and implements, apart from the tribal context, they may be simple instruments, extensions of people's limbs and desires as Robert Ardrey once edified describing weapons and tools. The important part of the relationship, however, was that all things were alive, and consequently their own power and wisdom was incorporated with them wherever they were represented. Modern humans use weapons, tools, and instruments to extend the capabilities of their own selves, and they use these things mechanically. Tribal people in using their instruments did not simply extend the scope of their own capabilities, but enhanced their abilities through the addition of the powers inherent in the relationships they had with other living things.

Today we attend colleges and universities in order to learn the principles of how things work and how to use instruments properly. Tribal people learned these things in religious ceremonies, depending on the intensity and scope of the vision a person received, or the frequency with which spirits informed him or her concerning the proper attitude to take when exercising certain powers. Thus, it was a holistic understanding that undergirded tribal technology, and use of the technology was vision-specific. That is to say, the knowledge the old ones attached to their technology demanded that they use their powers sparingly and on the proper occasions. A person could not indiscriminately use powers as we casually use our instruments today. This lesson is important because today with modern technology we tend to believe that we can apply it on a rather indiscriminate basis, and we are learning that often we do not really understand the side effects such use creates.

The old anthropology and history of religious schools used to paint tribal peoples as a superstitious lot who cringed in fear of the natural elements and made up simplistic explanations for all things they did not understand in an effort to create some kind of science for themselves. Modern science tends to use two kinds of questions to examine the world: (1) "How does it work?" and (2) "What use is it?" These questions are natural for a people who think the world is constructed to serve their purposes. The old people might have used these two questions in their effort to understand the world, but it is certain that they always asked an additional question: "What does it mean?"

HEALING THE LACK OF BALANCE

The old people, surveying a landscape, had such a familiarity with the world that they could immediately see what was not in its place. If they discerned anything that seemed to be out of its natural order—a nocturnal animal in the daytime, unusual clouds or weather conditions, or a change of the plants—they went to work immediately to discover what this change meant. Many observers have said that this ability to perceive anomalies meant that the people could see when nature was out of balance, and I certainly would not quarrel with this characterization. When the people saw an imbalance, their understanding of the natural ordering of cosmic energies informed them that their responsibility was to initiate ceremonies that would help bring about balance once again.

Eventually it was recognized that the world had a moral being and that disruptions among human societies created disharmony in the rest of the world. This belief corresponded to modern professional ethics but differed from them in that the whole tribal society was involved in healing the lack of balance. Today it is only the professional who sees the imbalance, and the general society comes to believe that the scientist can create the technology needed to bring balance back again. Thus, in spite of a clearly deteriorating physical world brought about by industrial society, we still think in mechanical, technological terms when we discuss restoration of what we have disrupted. Because no one actually "sees" quantum waves, what is quantum physics except scientific mysticism?

Traditional technology may seem outdated to many Indian students now undertaking a scientific education. If so, they are not getting the full story from historians and apologists of science. It is said that Albert Einstein had holistic and sometimes substantial visions of the world, and that he spent most of his life looking for the proper mathematics to describe what he had experienced. One need only look at the many instances in which noted scientists had visions or dreams that solved the problem they were confronting. The world in which we live, at its very foundations, is unified and cannot be reduced by techniques and rationality. Where traditional Indians and modern science are quite different is in what they do with their knowledge after they have obtained it. Traditional people preserve the whole vision, and scientists generally reduce the experience to its alleged constituent parts and inherent principles. These principles then become orthodoxy and stumbling blocks to future generations.

A great gulf exists between these two ways of handling knowledge. Science *forces* secrets from nature by experimentation, and the results of the experiments are thought to be knowledge. The traditional peoples *accepted* secrets from the rest of creation. Science leaves anomalies, whereas the unexplained in traditional technology is held as a mystery—accepted, revered, but not discarded as useless. Science operates in fits and starts because the anomalies of one generation often become the orthodoxy of the next generation—witness the continental drift theories, catastrophism, and the fictional theories about the Bering Strait.

GIVING TRADITIONAL
TECHNOLOGY A CAREFUL LOOK

Indian students would do well to understand the traditional approach to learning about the world in addition to taking the scientific courses to gain entrance to professions. They should be prepared in their work, as students and later as professional people, to answer the question "What does it mean?" in addition to answering any other questions that as professional people they will be expected to answer. Traditional technology can be extremely useful because it always reminds us that we must take our cue about the world from the experiences and evidence that the world gives us. We may elicit and force secrets from nature, but nature is only answering the specific questions we ask it. It is not giving us the whole story as it would if it were specifically involved in the communication of knowledge. What is given willingly is much more valuable than what is demanded as a matter of force.

Because many Indian students will be working for their tribes once they receive their professional degrees, it would benefit them to give traditional technology a careful look. Tribal lands and resources have always been used on a sustained-yield basis, and this attitude is in distinct contrast to the American propensity to exhaust resources for short-term gains. Modern technology might indeed be useful in repairing the damages already done to tribal lands so that the lands can once again be put on a traditional use pattern and become productive. And even this possibility can be learned from the world as it responds to ceremonies and human societies who understand their place in the larger cosmos. As science progresses, so do the ceremonies, and as we look ahead there is considerably more to be gained by combining insights than by ignoring them.

# TECHNOLOGICAL
# HOMELESSNESS

*D. Wildcat*

The United States is a nation of homeless people. A modest esti-mate would place three-fourths of U.S. citizens in a condition of homelessness: a technology-induced condition of homelessness. I am not talking about the desperate situation of the far too many Americans without any real means to provide for a domicile or residence with a definite address. These individuals and families have real problems, though their lack of housing, ironically, might be straightforwardly addressed and solved to a great extent given a little moral courage and political will. No, the problem of home-lessness demanding attention concerns the vast majority of Amer-icans today living in houses, condos, and apartments, residences with addresses, who have taken advantage of our society's modern education systems and technologies and still feel lost, disconnect-ed, ungrounded, or what we call homeless.

By *homeless,* I mean without a home as the *American Heritage Dictionary* secondarily defines *home:* "an environment or haven of shelter, of happiness and love." In industrial and postindustrial so-cieties, human beings, especially in U.S. suburbs, live less in shel-ters than bunkers, strategic enclaves where they do not so much live as primarily sleep. Happiness and sleep among those "with means" in America are only a pharmaceutical prescription away, and for those "without means" happiness is predictably defined by success in attaining the material wealth a great many of the un-happy "with means" possess. As for love, the line of a popular song states, "What's love got to do with it?" As it turns out, for many, very little.

It is disturbing to have to point these facts out, especially because we are surrounded by them daily. Alexis de Tocqueville, almost two centuries ago, feared for democracy in America because he saw Americans so preoccupied with material success that they had little time for participation in democracy. Only three decades after Tocqueville's assessment, Suquamish leader Seattle noted that human beings seemed to have lost the knowledge of how to live. By the middle of the nineteenth century Americans were already in a struggle for survival. The irony is obvious: we have learned more about the manipulation of the physical or material elements of the world for our human comfort and convenience, and yet American workers are experiencing increasing rates of anxiety, depression, and stress. Not surprisingly, in the last decade American workers have surpassed the Japanese in time spent working. The United States is now the longest-working advanced industrial nation in the world.

The economy may be good for some or even many, but good for what, or good at what? The answer is simple: making money. It is often quoted that after the successful detonation of the atomic bomb (the preeminent example of technological achievement in a scientistic worldview), Einstein lamented that everything had changed but the way human beings think. There is nothing new in the judgment that industrialization and manufacture have disproportionately benefited a few financially, and in terms of material comfort and convenience benefited many, although inequitably. But at what cost to ourselves and our ecological communities? Indices and rates of mental illness are all up, especially when one includes those illnesses labeled neuroses. Ironically, it appears we may have bought more with the materialist mantra of comfort than we bargained for—a significant amount of discomfort to our spirits.

In the Western tradition the critique of industrialization has largely been over the control and management of the system of production, and consequently, the distribution of the industrial economy's benefits. Apart from a neglected anarchist moral critique and a recent strain of criticism referred to as neo-Ludditism, only a few have questioned the overall effects of technology on the human condition and on how we live, and what it means to be a human being.

I wish all young Indian students would read Stan Steiner's *The New Indians*. It documents a history too few Indian students today know. They should at least read the foreword, in which Steiner recounts the following incident. In the 1960s Vine Deloria, Jr. was invited to a civil rights fund-raiser to see how things were done. As the event was winding down the topic of Red Power was raised, and the featured keynote speaker laughed and quickly dismissed the notion, to which Deloria replied:

> Red Power will win. We are no longer fighting for physical survival. We are fighting for ideological survival. Our ideas will overcome your ideas. We are going to cut the country's whole value system to shreds.
>
> It isn't important that there are only 500,000 of us Indians. What is important is that we have a superior way of life. We Indians have a more human philosophy of life. We Indians will show this country how to act human. Someday this country will revise its constitution, its laws, in terms of human beings, instead of property. If Red Power is to be a power in this country it is because it is ideological.

When told again that Indians should be fighting for equality and civil rights, not Red Power, Deloria continued:

> We do. But that isn't the question. The question is, What is the nature of life? It isn't what you eat, or whether you eat, or who you vote for, or whether you vote, or not. What is the ultimate value of a man's life? That is the question.

To linear thinkers the above statements may seem out of place in a discussion of technology, but they are the most fundamental questions to be considered as we think of the development and use of technology: to what ultimate end or purpose are these tools?

Education today must now undertake a serious examination of these questions, and there is no better place to begin than classrooms in American Indian communities. Here, there still exists an experiential metaphysics and worldview that approaches technology as essentially a question of nature and how we human beings live with and in nature.

For the sake of clarification, I submit that two very different understandings of technology are the issue. A deeply seated (metaphysically based) Western view of technology as science applied to industrial (manufacture) and commercial objectives, versus a (metaphysically based) American Indian, or rather indigenous, view of technology as practices and toolmaking to enhance our living in and with nature. The Western conception and practices of technology are bound up in essentially human-centered materialism: the doctrine that physical well-being and worldly possessions constitute the greatest good and highest value in life. Indigenous conceptions and practices of technology are embedded in a way of living life that is inclusive of spiritual, physical, emotional, and intellectual dimensions emergent in the world or, more accurately, particular places in the world.

We cannot afford to minimize or soft-sell the situation in which we find ourselves. The problems we most likely, and certainly our children and grandchildren, will face are monumental: environmental degradation, technological imperialism, consumerism for consumerism's sake (what Thorstein Veblen called conspicuous consumption), and increasing social dysfunction. Yet there is reason to be cautiously optimistic, because we have literally reached a place, or I should say places, in the modern world where the plethora of problems that surround us are rising to level where they cannot be ignored.

Nevertheless, there is hope for our children because, in spite of what some of humankind has sought to improve and control in the natural world, tremendous beauty and wisdom are still around us. The challenge of indigenous education is to expand the ability of children to experience the world—the world they are a part of as their home, an environment or refuge of happiness (with hard work) and love (with respect). We can and must educate a generation of children who find home in the landscapes and ecologies they inhabit.

As we make great strides in ecological knowledge at the beginning of the twenty-first century, the problem human beings face today is simply summed up by the following question: "What exactly is the ecological niche of human beings?" Although scientists have painstakingly sought to classify and analyze all the other life-forms on our planet, it strikes me as odd that they have spent so little time considering just what our (human beings') "niche" might be.

Many of us human beings have sought to distinguish ourselves from the rest of nature, but to what end, what purpose? Human beings in modern Western civilization have historically identified culture as the primary feature distinguishing us from other animals. Specifically, toolmaking, or technology, and language have until very recently been thought to clearly demarcate us, humans, from them, other animals. Some of us have found great solace in thinking of ourselves, with our culture, as above other animals and the natural world in general.

It is this human "cultural context" that must be placed in a broader understanding of natural "history" if we are to understand ourselves; and within culture, technology must be carefully scrutinized. Indigenous American Indian traditions, we believe, are our best guides for reassessing technology, for they represent practical ways of seeing technology as a part of nature.

It is difficult for many adults in modern American industrial or postindustrial society to understand that the natural world—and to be precise, local ecosystems—ought to play a major role in determining the technologies we employ. The examples are so obvious in hindsight—I repeat, in hindsight—that we would do well to pause before we leap headlong into the bioengineering utopia we are presently being promised.

Living close to the confluence of the Kansas and Missouri rivers for the last three decades, it has been interesting to watch people's reaction in the 1990s to having, within the span of several years, two 500-hundred-year floods. Dams and levees, while good for urban development and large agribusiness, are overall ill-conceived given the degradation to riparian ecosystems and water quality, not to mention the flood damage and costs to the federal government.

Dakota anthropologist Bea Medicine has discussed the destruction to sustainable Dakota agricultural practices that ensued with the damming of the Missouri River on the Standing Rock Sioux reservation. Wisely, the Dakota farmed in the rich river bottoms but set up their villages above them. They knew better than to set up villages on the river's edge, although in fair weather there was no obstacle to camping there. No synthetic fertilizers were needed, for when the floods came as they surely would, the soil would be enriched and replenished. Likewise, there were no damages to human-made dams, levees, and domiciles.

My friend and colleague Cynthia Annette, a riparian ecologist, likes to say, "Rivers have memories." No matter where we (humans) want them to go, they remember ancient paths. The Dakota knew this and chose to live in a manner that respected the Missouri River's memory. The counterpoint to this understanding is the U.S. Army Corps of Engineers, who have never met a river they could not dam. Compared to genetic engineering, building dams and levees to control rivers ought to be relatively easy, but rivers are hard to control. All the variables that combined to produce the incredible flooding, we are now told, could not have been predicted. In short, nature and the rivers had their way. The notion that technology can translate into control of nature is, as stated earlier, nothing more than—to borrow a phrase, if turnabout is fair play— a mythology, although a very modern one.

TECHNOLOGY IN THE BIG PICTURE

"Bridging Gaps in Technology and Culture." This was the theme at the 1998 Hazardous Waste Research Conference, where I suggested to scientists and engineers they address this problem by first acknowledging a complex set of interrelations in a formula I called TC3. Technology, community, communication, and culture are intimately related. Try to imagine any one of the four existing among human beings without the other three—you cannot. I summarized this relationship for scientists and engineers as the TC3 formula.

Haskell Environmental Research Studies Center programs and projects over the last five years have reminded me of the importance of the TC3 formula because unfortunately, most Americans live as if this relationship is unknown. That we speak of gaps in or between technology and culture is crucial, for it is symptomatic of a serious obstacle to understanding. These gaps obscure the reality that technology is a part of culture as are the forms that community and communication assume. Still, the recognition that gaps exist suggests the issue is far from academic. Rather, the issue strikes at the core of how we ought to think about technology and what education and environmental research ought to be about today: the way we live and our respect for the places where we live (our homes and communities). The advantage of Deloria's power-and-place-equal-personality equation is that when applied to technology, it forces one to frame technology in the big picture.

Many scholars, scientists, and engineers are engaged in problem solving and research as if TC3 were unimportant. Disciplinary boundaries and professional specialization force many to work in conceptual boxes, and we increasingly live literally in isolated/insulated physical boxes. The result is a natural and social forgetfulness about the way in which technology, community, communication, and culture are related. Collectively our human ancestors may very well have possessed a wisdom modern human societies desperately need—a wisdom not produced by superior "intelligence" or rationality, but born of direct experience and subsequent reflection. The wisdom resides in the recognition that the modern dichotomy between human/social issues versus technology/technical issues is a false one, an invidious distinction. Technology and humanity are as inseparable as human beings are from their natural environments.

Reading human history, one is impressed by the extent to which it is full of humankind's self-declared superiority. However, most

recent entries appear to revolve around technological achievements. For good reason: human evolution has resulted in an attribute that is anything but physical or adaptive as it is ordinarily
conveyed in beginning biology courses. Our uniqueness, as a
species, is found in the ability to use technology to live in environments that would otherwise be largely uninhabitable by humans
and the societies on which we depend.

Our capacity to manipulate environmental elements to com-
pensate for our physiological awkwardness is what nature has
given us two-legged persons to work with to secure our lives. It
appears natural selection has not selected us for a particular niche
or place on the planet, but has selected traits that have allowed
human beings, with the use of technology, to adapt to different
places and environments on our Mother Earth.

Central among those traits is our sociability or social nature.
Unlike the social dimension found in many animals—for example,
big cats, wolves, bears, dolphins, and of course higher primates—
our physiological awkwardness dictates a necessity for toolmaking
and manipulation absent among other animal species. This is less
a sign of human superiority than a sign of biological difference. In
my mind this explains why in our traditional indigenous ways of
speaking and praying we so often describe ourselves as pitiful beings. Humans depend on many good relations and relatives to live
and survive in this world—hardly superstition, just ecological fact.
Nature, nurture, and technology are intimately connected.

Our American Indian societies understood this profoundly important point: our evolutionary past has not made human beings
superior but merely different. We identify our culture or social
spheres as what distinguishes us from other biological life, but with
respect to other animals this is less a case of absolute uniqueness
than an issue of degree. Elizabeth Marshall Thomas has demonstrated this in her wonderful book *Tribe of the Tiger*. Yet it is the
degree to which our social behavior revolves around the development of technology that distinguishes us from other animals and
explains why we should consider technology as central to human
nature and history. We ought to give up on our modern notions of

human superiority, lest our technological "successes," as typically measured, become our defeat and the destruction of our home—the earth's biosphere—and many of the relatives we share it with.

From primitive toolmaking to the advent of modern machinery, our primary goal was to fashion material culture—clothing, shelter, utensils, and so on—that provided a social and cultural adaptation to environments and places. Throughout most of human history, places and environments shaped and limited the kinds of cultures humans created. Places, technologies, and cultures were inextricably connected.

Deloria's power-and-place-equal-personality equation, or P3 formula, makes for a spatial metaphysics of experience. The TC3 expression, technology, community, communication, and culture, is an attempt to identify the natural cultural feature of human beingness. P3 and TC3 are not rigorous mathematical expressions; rather, I think of both as symbolic expressions that can serve as mnemonic devices that preclude thinking of technology, or for that matter any of the key features of human culture, as outside of nature.

Our biologically and geographically diverse natural environments shaped how we lived—our livelihood activities, shelters, clothing, and much of our symbolic nonmaterial culture. Keith Basso's book *Wisdom Sits in Places* brilliantly documents the extent to which Western Apache history is less about time than places, or what might be called a sense of place.

New technologies have given humans the ability to reshape environments and geographies to accommodate comfort and convenience. And we are increasingly preoccupied with the physical rearrangement, manipulation, or engineering of natural environments. John Locke set out the rationale for this mode of living 300 years ago. In Locke's philosophy the rest of nature existed ultimately for humankind's benefit and convenience. It was a short step to reason that if natural environments do not meet our human standards of comfort, convenience, and aesthetic beauty, we ought to change them to do so.

Modern technology allows us to do precisely this, but at what cost? I believe the cost is a growing absence of a sense of place for human communities and correspondingly modern culture, which are literally "groundless." Thirty years ago Vine Deloria, Jr., described modern societies as rushing to create an "Artificial Universe." Vine Deloria may be one of the few nontechnical scholars unsurprised by discussions about artificial intelligence, globalization, and virtual "realities," "communities," "persons," and so forth. Human beings fail to experience the world as our ancestors did, and as many of my living indigenous elders do, because our technologies increasingly insulate us from direct experience and the acquisition of experiential knowledge from natural environments.

Automobiles, television, air conditioning, and computers, to pick four obvious examples, result in human convenience, entertainment, comfort, and escape from incredible drudgery. But I interact less directly and physically in time and space with other human beings and the natural environment because of the ease, comfort, privacy or relative isolation with which I can use these technologies. Technology, in general, has reshaped most people's everyday lives, often in measurably positive ways. But here is the irony: as we disengage technology from communities (which include plants, animals, and geographic/geologic features) with a sense of place, and thereby create cultures and forms of communication that are relatively abstract, we unconsciously destroy conditions for our human survival and threaten the lives of many other plants and animals with whom we share this biosphere.

I am not anti-technology; my human nature dictates otherwise. But my nature also requires community (nurture), and currently we pose the quest for community and new technologies as if they were mutually exclusive endeavors. They are not. This knowledge ought to give us reason to pause, not because of fear for what technologies literally do, but out of concern for their residual effects: the unintended byproducts of our human use of the technology.

Fortunately, there is some promise in the fact that we are beginning to have powerful allies in the dominant and mainstream system of education. Leading educators, child psychologists, and psychiatrists recently endorsed a report by the Alliance for Childhood, "Fool's Gold: A Critical Look at Computers in Childhood," and signed a petition suggesting "an immediate moratorium on the further introduction of computers in early childhood and elementary education."

It might be hoped that adults take notice of what extended computer-time does to them. A study by scientists at Carnegie Mellon University found that as individuals increased time on computers, they also increased feelings of loneliness and depression. What does it tell us when the high-tech interconnectivity of "webs" and "nets" leaves us feeling disconnected? It tells us that technology is potentially impoverishing and harmful to the soul, to our spiritual and interior lives that are formed by the number of good relations we acknowledge and maintain.

If we human beings begin our understanding of the natural world with the big picture, we must acknowledge our relatively recent arrival to our Mother Earth's biosphere. The result ought to be a kind of biological modesty, for many of our biosphere community members have been here much longer than we have. In the minds of many scientists, such as Richard Leaky, some of our biosphere neighbors may outlive us. Our traditional indigenous cultures are literally grounded in the geographies and natural environments to which we are historically connected. In fact, history itself, and our worldviews, philosophy, and material culture, were and in varying degrees still are shaped by a sense of place. If human beings continue to live as if ecology and evolution have given us a privileged place in the natural order of things, our human history may very well be a footnote in the life story of our Mother Earth.

It would be an ancient coyote story writ large if the technology human beings used to ensure our physical and material comfort and convenience resulted in no place to live on this planet—an ultimate form of homelessness that resulted in our extinction. We can bridge the technology and culture gap if we are willing not only to acknowledge the TC3 relationship but also to change the way we live. Human survival and the survival of many of our relatives may depend on it.

# TRANSITIONAL
# EDUCATION

*V. Deloria*

Education has a transitional function of moving individuals from one status or condition to another. In the old days we used to mark these transitions by giving the individual a new name, a name that would more accurately summarize his or her achievements. Today we award certificates, diplomas, and degrees to mark each step the student takes. But education itself is transitional. New theories and concepts are continually intruding into established patterns of teaching and institutional organization so that the experience of education changes radically from generation to generation. For American Indians there is an additional element to be considered, because Indian school systems are at best transitory. There is no predictability in the actions of Congress that would reassure the people that a decent education will always be available to them. Indian education is conceived to be a temporary expedient for the purpose of bringing Indians out of their primitive state to the higher levels of civilization. Presumably, when this ill-defined status is reached there will be no more use for special programs in Indian education.

The goal of much of modern education seems to be socialization. That is to say, with some few exceptions, we are training people to present an acceptable profile to the corporate industrial world. Our undergraduate degrees actually certify that the student has a smattering of knowledge about a number of fields, is fairly well acquainted with one particular field, and can accommodate himself or herself to institutional life. We pretend otherwise, but this goal is what we actually have in mind. Indian education is somewhat unique in that it has always been premised upon the idea of assimilation without regard to socialization. From the very beginning, first missionaries and later government teachers sought to erase the cultural backgrounds of Indian children with the naive belief that once a vacuum was created, Western social mores and beliefs would naturally rush in to replace long-standing tribal practices and customs.

A review of Indian education programs of the past three decades will demonstrate that they have been based upon very bad expectations. In 1960 there were approximately 2,000 Indians in higher education, financed primarily by private scholarship funds and individual and family efforts. In 2000 best estimates show that we have something like 70,000 Indians in various forms of higher education, financed by a bewildering variety of sources, including colleges and universities, private groups, state scholarships, and several forms of federal assistance. In spite of our continual complaints, it should be obvious that Indian education has made some major progress since 1960, and that while funds are hard to come by for many students, the overall picture appears very bright.

Yet we are all discontented with what is happening in Indian education and we cannot quite put our finger on why. The majority of funds in Title IV and other programs have concentrated on the sciences and administration and management, and yet, as we look around at both reservation programs and the distribution of Indians in private industry, we find little evidence that the efforts of the last forty years have made a difference. We still need many Indian educational administrators, we have a pressing need for management personnel, and we still have great difficulty finding Indians working in industry. Reservation and border-town schools appear to be falling even farther behind the national norms, and many schools are simply thinly disguised holding pens to keep the young people institutionalized during the day until they reach a certain age when we can demand that they behave like adults. The outbreak of devil worship on some reservations and the growing drug problems on others demonstrate the inadequacy of the present situation.

## So What Problem Are We Actually
## Facing and How Do We Deal with It?

Education has generally been misunderstood by its practitioners. It is defined as both process and content, and it is exceedingly difficult to tell from educational behavior and philosophy whether or not the educator is making the proper distinctions. We can divide Indian education into two basic periods: the period of content and the period of process. From the beginning of the Republic, in fact from the beginning of contact, education was primarily a matter of providing content, new ways of thinking of things and new facts. From the Meriam Report of 1928 until the present we have been living in the age of process—which is to say, we have been more concerned with *how* children learn than with *what* they learn. During the past forty years we have been exclusively concerned with how they learn and have almost studiously avoided asking what it is they are learning.

This situation is particularly difficult for students who are studying science because, in most respects, science is content and not process. Consequently, after educating Indian young people in schools that stress learning experiences, we suddenly place upon them the demand that they accommodate themselves to the scientific enterprise—which is to say, build scientific expertise on a secondary education that has very little content. The student has no choice except to attempt to learn the scientific curriculum as well as gain background in the mass of conflicting ideas that now passes for Western civilization. When the social adjustment from Indian community-based culture to non-Indian urban networking culture has to be made at the same time, many students adopt a very rigid posture concerning personal, group, and community values. Too often they model themselves after the professionals in their academic field or their institutional situation. This adjustment then forces them outside their Indian circle and greatly inhibits their ability to draw from their own tribal traditions the lessons that could be profitably learned regarding both science and the social world in which they live. That we are producing any Indians in science at all is a tribute to the perseverance of this generation of Indian young people.

Where then do we start to make changes in Indian education so that we can deal with the problems we perceive? Perhaps the first step we can take is to admit that education is transitional and that it has both a beginning and an end. Indian education must certainly begin within the Indian community, be it a reservation, small town, or urban setting. Recent legislation, most notably the Indian Education Act, has attempted to deal with this, beginning by requiring that schools receiving federal funds have Indians on their school boards and advisory committees. Here Indians were placed within the process of education but not allowed to determine its content. In Indian survival schools, Indians were allowed to determine the content but were generally isolated from the process of education. Consequently, few schools at the primary and secondary levels have been able to do very much about improving education as a whole.

When we look closely at the idea of a transitional process, we must note that the goal or result should have been contained within the beginning and should flow directly out of it as the potential to be realized. The old Indians saw this necessity at once. The famous saying of Sitting Bull, basically that the people should take what is good of the white person and reject what is bad, assumed from the start that Indians would begin in, and always have recourse to, their own communities and cultural traditions. The missing element here, or rather the conclusion that we always avoid drawing, is the context in which education occurs. Context is also the beginning; it is not only the place to start, it is the channel within which all other developments must occur. Modern Indian education too often looks at the present poverty context of Indian communities and then devises programs that are supposed to deal with and overcome the handicaps that present conditions contain. Thus we have educational programs for every conceivable kind of social and community handicap and disability. But the products of these programs are often worse for the wear, and the best students emerging from them represent but a very small percentage of the total student population.

Compensatory programs fail because they take the Indian context as the immediate conditions under which Indians live. This analysis is a common characteristic of the Western way of thinking, but it is certainly not a traditional Indian way of thought, nor is it the manner in which many Indian parents conceive of education or of their lives. In politics we always speak about the coming generations, and anthologies are filled with clever sayings and quotations about the lands of our grandparents and the next generation of Indians. The essence of these sayings is a view of the world that encompasses many generations of people. That is to say, the proper context of Indian education should be whatever existing conditions are plus the traditional manner in which the tribe has faced its difficulties. In other words, the proper context is the history and culture of the tribe, regardless of the present location of its membership.

We do not have good present examples of how Indian education has worked when the context defined both the content and the process of education, but the school systems of the Five Civilized Tribes certainly functioned in this manner—and they functioned very well indeed. Tribal college graduates could generally speak their own language and English, and they had a reading knowledge of a European language. These were school systems designed by the tribes themselves, funded by the tribes through annuity accounts in the federal treasury, and staffed and operated by tribal governments. The Creek school system invented the school warrant system of finance that was adopted by a good many of the non-Indian school districts in the western states in succeeding years. Additionally, the Five Tribes had seminaries that educated the young women of the tribe and orphanages to take care of the homeless children.

We have part of the message of the Five Tribes educational system today—tribal control—but we do not have the tribal concern to make education the primary function of the tribal government. In those days tribal officials made an annual visit to each school in the tribal system. Students were expected to recite what they had learned in order to demonstrate that they had mastered the content of what was taught. Scholarships for higher education were not handed out on a tribal membership basis. Students had to earn tribal support after their secondary school days were completed. At graduation whole families came to the school and listened to the students demonstrate their knowledge of the various subjects they had studied. The old tribal custom of reciting deeds done on war parties was translated wholly into a recitation of schoolwork completed. School graduations were the big social event of the year. When we try to summarize the basic philosophy of these schools, we find that there was a general belief that education was something for the tribe, not for the individual. School became an integral part of tribal customs. It was not something imposed on the people.

It is not possible for tribes to fund their own schools today. Indeed, most American communities do not support their own schools but receive federal, state, county, and private financial assistance so that, to a certain degree, no school district in the United States has the financial freedom to determine either the process or the content of its education. Funding is not the issue, however. The issue is providing the context in which what is taught and the processes by which it is taught make sense. Here tribes have a very decided advantage over non-Indian school districts. An individual is a tribal member all his or her life, and consequently the tribe always has a central core constituency of people who represent the individual's interest. Non-Indian communities, on the other hand, are hardly what a person could truly call communities. Apart from small towns that have a greater resemblance to Indian tribes than to other non-Indian communities, most American cities and suburbs are merely places through which people travel. It is an exceedingly rare non-Indian who lives in the same town where his or her grandparents spent their adult lives. As a result, non-Indian communities are themselves in transition. That is to say, they lack context, and consequently their educational programs are increasingly educating fewer and fewer people.

Without a context, science quickly becomes a technology, the application of theory to practical use without so much as a thought about the consequences of the application. This process has been determining the fate of American communities for most of this century, but now with increasing scientific knowledge we are coming to the end of the period when we can thoughtlessly apply science. In the next decade we will see a massive backlash by ordinary citizens against the use of technology for corporate and private profit, in defiance of the health and living conditions of people in affected areas. A quick reading of any magazine or newsletter devoted to ecological issues, civil rights, animal rights, or agricultural concerns will reveal the scope of the modern reform movement. In short, for the first time since the beginning of the American industrial revolution, which probably began in the 1880s, Americans are now trying to build a context in which the content of education will have some value.

Indian education can exercise an enormous amount of influence in the future if we can place it once again within the tribal context. Almost every book now published by the New Age movement is crammed full of sayings by Indians to the effect that the earth's resources are limited, to the effect that people should have priority, and to the effect that there is an important spiritual dimension to human life, that human life has definite meaning that transcends the technological world in which we find ourselves. All of this attention is merely the exploration by non-Indians of windows into the Indian understanding of the universe. There is a deeply held belief that by appropriating a few wise sayings of Indians, longstanding problems brought about by the misuse of science and greedy capitalism can be solved. But merely appropriating ideas only provides slogans, not understanding.

Until the present time, the theory underlying Indian education was that it would provide a transitional process for turning the Indian child into an acceptable citizen. Education thus moved from an Indian context into a condition where the original context, the Anglo-Saxon Protestant world, was itself eroding because it was adopting an education of process and not content. If we now see the fallacy in this process and redefine Indian education as an internal Indian institution, an educational process that moves within the Indian context and does not try to avoid or escape this context, then our education will substantially improve. It will originate as part of the tribal perspective about life and pick up additional information on its return to Indian life.

Establishing the Indian context, in view of the absence of clearly defined tribal goals and philosophies, can be easily done by present Indian students. The primary question they should ask themselves is whether or not what they are learning will have some meaning to tribal people. And the answer, at first glance, will be a resounding "No." We presently do not know how to bring knowledge and information back to the tribe because we have not paid sufficient attention to the history and culture of our people. We have been deluded into thinking that there is no applicability of information on behalf of the tribe or no possibility of making our knowledge meaningful. So we must use what we learn about the scientific understanding of the world to ask questions of our people about how our ancestors understood the world, remembering that the tribe exists over many generations and possesses a cumulative knowledge that transcends any particular generation.

The answers that we will receive, when we ask elders and when we read recorded accounts of beliefs and practices, will often seem strange and many times irreconcilable with our scientific knowledge. But we must not use the scientific method to determine the truth or falsity of our comparison. We must learn to place the difference within the tribal context and there reconcile conflicting points of view. As Indians we know some things because we have the cumulative testimony of our people. We *think* we know other things because we are taught in school that they are true. The proper transition in Indian education should be the creative tension that occurs when we compare and reconcile these two perspectives.

# INDIGENIZING POLITICS
# AND ETHICS:
# A REALIST THEORY

*D. Wildcat*

Transitional education challenges us to establish a "creative tension" as we compare and reconcile, where possible, Western scientific knowledge and information with our own cumulative tribal wisdom. As we prepare to think about political sovereignty as an educational initiative, I can think of no better creative tension to explore than that between Western political models and an indigenous American Indian conception of politics and ethics.

American public policy making and administration are informed by a whole set of principles and concepts entrenched in the worldview of Western civilization. They are based on principles, categories, and relationships that are unconscious and seldom questioned. Unless we explore practical public policy issues facing American Indians from entirely different worldview or, more specifically, from a widely shared foundation (what Deloria calls metaphysics) of indigenous North American worldviews, we will continue to make many social problems worse. And we will continue to fall short of democratic promises far removed from classical social contract theory. Public policy makers, managers, scientists, and the general public might gain much by developing policies and practices for human societies based on an indigenous model of politics and ethics, which builds on an American Indian metaphysics of place and power.

The indigenous theory of public policy making and administration offered here comes from what I will call a protoscientific understanding of the natural world: an understanding based on human experience and empirical trial and error found in "the cumulative testimony of our people." In order to understand this indigenously grounded theory of politics and ethics, three key premises must be explored and understood.

First, public policy issues in Native worldviews involve consideration for the rights or we might say more accurately, following Deloria, the "personalities" of plants, animals, and the physical features of the natural world—for example, land, air, and water—as well as our relationships among our humankind. This is not a naive or romantic premise, for if considered with the full force of its implications, it will be understood as signaling a profound shift in awareness. In the eyes of most modern peoples immersed in America's modern industrial consumer society, it will, according to their Western worldview, entail an "irrational" sacrifice on the part of humankind. Of course, seen through the eyes of traditional Native peoples, today's governmental policies, especially natural resource and energy policies, seem unwise or unsustainable at best and at their worst comparable to a biological holocaust.

Second, the goals of this indigenous theory are practical and utilitarian in a sense akin to Aristotle's *summum bonum;* however, as emphasized above, the framework for the measurement of the *summum bonum,* or the "greatest good," is not human society but the ecosystem or natural environment that forms one's political and ethical community in the broadest sense. In short, the Native view advocates an understanding of the public sphere, which includes many persons, including many other-than-human persons. In fact, it seems to me that Deloria's proposal to understand place and power as the central features of an American Indian metaphysics perfectly grounds the theory I am offering for exploration.

Third, and contrary to many misinterpretations of Native worldviews, nearly all indigenous North American worldviews that I am familiar with consider the world as dynamic, not static. These views acknowledge the biological and physical principles of emergence—especially in their accounts of creation—which on the whole are much less anthropocentric and much more ecological and evolutionary (albeit in a sense not reducible to popular genetic models) than classical Western accounts of creation, whether Greek, Roman, or Judeo-Christian.

The ideas presented here are the collective cultural wisdom of the many indigenous peoples I have had the good fortune to study with and, most importantly, live with during my last sixteen years at Haskell Indian Nations University. I am merely synthesizing what has become obvious to me and many other American Indian scholars: that a foundation for an indigenous practice and theory of politics and ethics exists. Fortunately, at a general conceptual level this indigenous foundation for politics and ethics can be conveyed by comparison with what easily counts as the foundation of Western political theory and ethics: Aristotle's *Politics* and *The Nicomachean Ethics*.

## Aristotle's Politics and Ethics

Two key insights shape Aristotle's thought: first, the recognition that humans are by nature political animals; and second, the understanding that ethics are the result of custom and habit. Politics, for Aristotle, is understood as the study of social arrangements, whereby individual human virtues are developed to their fullest. Inquiry into ethics is defined by Aristotle as the study of the greatest good within social arrangements or relationships. Aristotle's genius is in the implicit linking of politics to ethics.

Aristotle correctly recognizes that human beings are by nature political, or social, animals, but this does not imply that human beings are "by nature" ethical in their behavior. If not born ethical actors, Aristotle rightly concludes one's ethics will be a result of learning through experience in a community—through inculcation by custom and habit. On this point, Aristotle's reliance on the formation of values and beliefs through societal experience, as opposed to a system of ethical values produced through teaching or preaching, has a great affinity with American Indian thinking about the source of ethics. *God Is Red* pointed out that the strength of American Indian value systems, including ethics, is found in the context of their "communities"—the natural environments from which they emerge. Aristotle's emphasis on the state, custom and habit, and the greatest good provides the basis for a comparison to an American Indian or indigenous conception of politics and ethics.

In Aristotle's logic all things move toward their natural end, that end being the full development of the essence of that thing: the revealing of its real nature. He contends the essence of being human involves our ability to reason. However, because this ability to reason (to make choices) regarding what we ought to do is only fully developed in the context of society, it is necessary that the study of ethics leads to the study of politics. Aristotle believed that a human being, either unable to live in or without need of society, "must be either a beast or a god: he is not a part of a state. A social instinct is implanted in all men by nature.... For man, when perfected is the best of animals, but when separated from law and justice, he is the worst of all" (*Politics*, Book I).

Human nature leads to the creation of society, but the form that society takes is not determined by the nature of human beings. If it were, we would not see the diversity of social arrangements and phenomena throughout the world we today identify as culture.

Aristotle's recognition of diversity in human virtue and various forms of the state also facilitates a comparison to American Indian politics and ethics. Aristotle's empiricism leads him to pose both human virtue and the structure of the state as complex totalities reflective of each other. He never loses sight of the fact that virtue for human beings is manifold, with many different forms and specific practices composing the totality of what is understood as virtuous.

His treatment of virtue as complex allows him to see the state as the institutional embodiment of the greatest good—the *summum bonum*. For the greatest combination or sum of virtues making up the *summum bonum* can only be found in the state, which exists to allow all individuals to fulfill their virtue to the fullest, whether they be slave, servant, soldier, or musician. A virtuous leader and a good state are those that allow every individual person to develop their unique share of virtue to the fullest for accomplishment of the greatest good.

Nevertheless, Aristotle does suggest a hierarchy of values. He clearly determines the virtue of a ruler superior to the subject, and likewise, freeman compared to slave, adult male compared to female and child. He also indicates slaves are slaves by nature and rulers are rulers by nature. Aristotle's worldview is not one with equal opportunity with respect to virtue. While his theory is at its weakest in the manner in which the complex totality of virtue is hierarchically divided, his idea that human virtue is complex and his hierarchical prejudices are clearly explained by the empiricism he adopts in lieu of following Plato's idealism.

Aristotle recognizes that each individual possesses some share or part of virtue, not some universal abstract conception of virtue. As no individual possesses identical or all shares of the complex totality that constitute human virtue, society becomes the site where human beingness is most fully recognized. Because communities, and ultimately states, arise from the nature of human beings, it follows that the structures of communities and states must necessarily reflect the complex and diverse totality of human virtue. Aristotle believes "the good" exists in every person realizing his or her essence or true nature. Because every human being has a different share of virtue, which can only be realized in society, then the organization of society ought to be directed toward all members of society, each and every person, realizing their respective virtue(s) to the fullest. In Aristotle's mind the function of the state must be to allow every person to realize her or his virtue to the fullest. Ethics and politics are inextricably bound together.

Aristotle's naturalistic moral element is implicit throughout his discussion of politics. The leadership of a society or state, regardless of whether it be the leadership of one, a few, or the many, ought to work toward the goal of realizing virtue in its full, manifold, complex totality—a complex and diverse totality of human virtues. Failure of the state to accomplish this goal merely reflects the corruption of human activities and organization.

In Aristotle's mind there is no single or ideal form of the state like Plato's *Republic*. Instead, numerous forms, good and bad, of the state exist, but in all cases the distinction between the good and the bad state is made according to the ability of the state and its leaders to allow all human beings therein to realize their share or part of virtue to the fullest. The distinction between a good state structure and its leader(s), and a corrupt state structure and its political leader(s), rises and falls with the ability of both leader and structure to allow all humans in society to develop their virtue to the fullest. Ethics and politics are inextricably linked in Aristotle's thought.

The key elements to Aristotle's political and ethical theory are human beings, the state, and the *summum bonum*. One can and ought to read Aristotle's reference to the "state" as government. Aristotle's experience in fourth-century Greece explains why he understood the state as the highest good of all. The city-state was the largest and most extensive social institution in Greece. Its formal creation of law and respect for custom and habit created the natural social environment for human development. Consequently, Aristotle sees the state as the institution "which embraces all the rest, aims at good in a greater degree than any other, and at the highest good" (*Politics,* Book I).

Aristotle recognizes that people require a social existence to be most fully human. He recognizes that social experience, primarily through custom and habit, plays a substantial role in shaping one's values and beliefs. Although born political, that is, social, animals, our ethics or lack thereof will necessarily be products of the society and political institutions that shape us. Therefore, the study of ethics—morality—entails the examination of the social arrangements and relations in which we find human beings. Although Aristotle's basic logic is similar to that underpinning indigenous North American politics and ethics, the terms of his theory are significantly different from indigenous theory.

A COMPARISON OF ARISTOTLE'S
IDEAS TO INDIGENOUS THOUGHT

Traditional Native thought agrees with Aristotle's linkage between an individual's ethical development and one's community. However, unlike Aristotle's treatment of the "state" or community, which consists exclusively of human beings, traditional Native thinkers include as a part of their political communities many other-than-human persons, including persons that swim, winged persons, four-legged persons, and so on. In short, while Western thought, following Aristotle's lead, defines politics and ethics as exclusively human issues and endeavors, Native thought and, more importantly, practices have defined politics and ethics as involving a much broader conception of persons. This point is obvious in the stories, oral traditions, and ceremonies and social life of Native peoples. Many of our languages even offer evidence in support of this claim.

In their earliest interactions with the Iroquois, French Jesuits recorded that the Iroquois seemed confused with respect to who or what constituted a person. The confusion was the Jesuits', not the Iroquois'. The Iroquois understood the concept of person, or personhood, to include plants, animals, and other natural features of their environment, and their language expressed this understanding. As a result, when they considered their moral and political community, it was perfectly reasonable to include the non- or other-than-human persons—plants, animals, and some other natural phenomena—as community members.

This very ancient idea is the basis of an implicit environmental ethos, an ethos that leads one to fundamentally different notions about how we ought to relate to the environment, apply technology, and generally live with the earth. The worldview attendant to this ethos requires one to speak of a moral sphere that goes beyond merely thinking that morality is about the relationships you and I have as human beings. Morality and politics have to do with a reality that involves relationships we have with other-than-human persons of the biosphere and the ecology we (human beings) are a part of.

Morality and politics require that we acquaint ourselves with the many personalities we interact with daily. Natural resource "managers," public policy makers, scientists, and the general public can gain much by developing policies and practices informed by this key feature of indigenous North American worldviews. The best illustration of how Native peoples include many other natural objects and living beings as members of their community is found in Native clan systems and totems. It is frustrating to constantly hear non-Native peoples speaking romantically of the Indians' "closeness to nature" or "love of nature." The relationship is more profound than most people can imagine, and the implications of this relationship will imply uncomfortable consequences for many. To be Wolf, Bear, or Deer clan means that you are kin to these other persons. These are known and understood as your relatives. As Onondaga elder Oren Lyons remarked during the twenty-fifth-anniversary Earth Day celebration in Washington, D.C.: "We don't call a tree a resource, we don't call the fish a resource. We don't call the bison a resource. We call them our relatives. But the general population uses the term resources, so you want to be careful of that term—resources for just you?"

A radical shift in awareness and behavior occurs when one no longer considers nature as full of resources but of relatives. Like all kinship relations certain obligations and rights are assumed with membership in a clan. The customs, habits, obligations, and rights that correspond with clan and special societies in our tribes served to constantly remind us of the complex community that shapes our identity and ensures our continued existence.

As Native peoples our clan identities and numerous ceremonies exist to, among other things, reinforce this awareness of our relatedness and connection to these other beings. We persons, inclusive of plant and animal persons and the human beings, are all related and connected. These are the so-called new insights of evolution, ecology, and environmental science, and they are the very ancient wisdom of our traditional elders or true indigenous scholars.

Because in nearly all of our Native creation stories animal and plant persons existed before human persons, these kin exist as our elders. These animal and plant elders, as much as our human elders, are our guides. They are members of our community. Aristotle proposed that our values—guiding how we ought to live—are learned from our fellow community members. From an indigenous perspective Aristotle's basic reasoning was right, but his notion of community and its members was wrong.

Native people would argue that it makes no sense to limit the notion of politics and ethics to only human beings. How we human beings live will indeed reflect the communities we belong to; however, by limiting the definition of *persons* to human beings, Aristotle created a false and far too narrow sense of community and corresponding spheres of political and moral life. The inclusion of other living beings and natural objects into a category of persons, which includes human beings, requires a notion of politics and ethics inclusive of these other community members.

The comparison to Aristotle can be further extended. Aristotle recognized that it took human beings with many different parts of virtue to make a community. Artists, builders, farmers, designers, and so on are all required to make a strong community. Each person has what I have chosen to call a different share of virtue. Today we often speak of personal/professional strengths and weaknesses—Aristotle's point is obvious: we are not all good at the same thing. All of us are much better at doing some things than others; in Aristotle's mind this is natural and to be expected. The manner in which Aristotle develops this idea to create a hierarchically divided sense of virtue is necessarily limited given the incompleteness and partiality of his observations.

As a result of Aristotle's limited experience he inevitably speaks of different virtues as more virtuous than others. However, if Aristotle's notion of virtue is treated as a complex totality, a concept with manifold parts, it seems to me that what is right about Aristotle's reasoning can be kept and what is wrong can be discarded.

Aristotle's argument seems reasonable, but he stopped short of seeing the big picture, as figure 1 illustrates. Replace the key elements of Aristotle's theory, humans beings, society, and the *summum bonum*, with American Indian conceptions of persons, ecosystems, and ecosystem sustainability or health, and you have a complex living system of politics and ethics.

According to Aristotle, it is the political and moral sphere of human existence that distinguishes human life from the rest of the natural life on earth. Aristotle was right to see the good state and the good leader(s) as those that allowed members to develop their

FIGURE 1—A Comparison: Aristotelian (Western) and Indigenous Politics and Ethics.

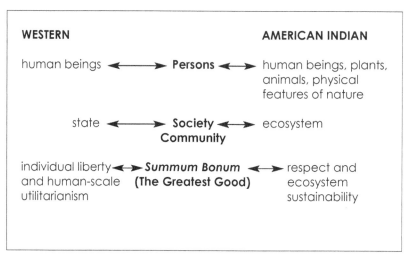

particular or shares of virtue to the fullest. However, from a Native standpoint, Aristotle stops short of grasping the big picture in a more accurate and immediate way. He too narrowly defines persons and community, or more properly the state. In so doing he poses a view of the greatest good that fairly ensures the environmental mess human beings have created. By excluding the many other-than-human persons of the natural world from active full participation in determination of the greatest good, ecological catastrophe seems guaranteed.

Whether intentional or not the result of this single idea has been to create a worldview where humans are thought to be above the rest of nature (superior by virtue of the fact that human evolution has resulted in our species possessing an intraspecies adaptive ability to reason), an idea that has brought us to the brink of a global ecological crisis by reducing the question, the very idea, of the *summum bonum* to be about relationships among human beings.

An indigenous conception of the *summum bonum* is rich and complex when compared to Aristotle's fairly simple conception of it. By analogy, the Iroquoian concept of personhood and community, as concisely summarized by John Mohawk in "Animal Natives Right to Survive," entails a concept of the greatest good that includes the four-legged persons, the winged persons, the persons that swim, and the plant persons. It is, in fact, more complex. The Iroquoian concept of the greatest good requires that human beings have more relationships, interdependencies, and persons to be attentive to when considering how to act—from a moral and political viewpoint—to realize the *summum bonum*. (John Mohawk, 1988).

I propose it is precisely this experiential insight that allows comparison to indigenous notions of relatedness and connectedness. Although a virtual cottage industry has developed among some scholars seeking to debunk any claim that Native peoples were unlike their recently arrived European neighbors in their interaction with their natural environment, it seems to me many have missed the crucial point. Our ancestors possessed technology, and they certainly used it to affect their environment. However, their use of technology was guided by an underlying premise that Bacon, Locke, Newton, and most modern engineers would have found incredible: our natural environments contain many more persons than our human selves, and these other-than-human persons are members of our political and ethical "community" and require respect.

Experience shaped Aristotle's and Native peoples' conceptions of politics and ethics. Aristotle's careful observations of human society led him to abandon a single ideal form of the state for a general theory that allowed for the particularity and diversity of various human situations and conditions. He concluded that the state was the highest expression of virtue because it constituted the site where the fullest expression of virtue could occur. The ethical dimension of the state was found in its character as the active and healthy combination of all virtues, or what I have called the manifold shares or parts of virtue as a complex totality. Indigenous thought suggests power does reside in the places and personalities that surround us. Consequently, possessing the power to do the right thing depends on understanding the entire ecosystem as the community in which virtue can be fully recognized in its complex totality.

Modern ecology and indigenous models of politics and ethics have much in common: they are both about the complex relationships between living organisms and their environments. Indigenous thought has, in my mind, one key advantage: it sees the ecosystem as the appropriate site for the study of politics and ethics. The error of Aristotle's thinking, and the great error of subsequent Western thinking about politics and ethics, is that it mistakenly and artificially takes human beings out of the community that in the most direct physical and spiritual sense our existence and identity depend on.

Not surprisingly, many non-Native environmentalists and ecologists have made the connection between biology, environment, and the very important questions about how we ought to live. What passes today as the science of ecology is nothing more than a restatement of very old Native North American concepts. Unfortunately, once again this has been treated as a great discovery— a little like the discovery of "America" some 500 years ago. To Native peoples this knowledge is not new, it is very ancient.

Although the scientific treatment of reality and the concepts that describe it are to some extent different, the knowledge of the physical attributes and relationships held by many traditional Natives is equivalent, if not superior, to the knowledge held by modern ecologists. It is superior primarily in the sense that traditional indigenous scholars operate minus the ideology that humans are somehow in their "unique" nature destined to live above the rest of the natural world.

The ideas offered here should not be misconstrued as suggesting (1) a carte blanche return to previous nonmodern ways of living or (2) a condemnation of all things modern, for it is neither. The suggestion is to evaluate the ideas independent of a simplistically abstract (in fact, idealist) linear view of history that sees Western civilization (including some of its "scientistic" practices) at the front or leading edge of history, with all other cultures behind and retarded, or behind and hoping to catch up.

A traditional American Indian view of politics and ethics facilitates understanding of a view of history that accords space or place at least as much importance in a conception of history as that given to time and chronology in Western civilization. What is thereby gained is an entire body of collective tribal experience—a foundation, really—that can serve to literally ground an education for life or living: a foundation shaping practices and thought that are more applicable to the issues we face on the planet today than the dominant Western model of politics and ethics, because it contains an inherent or implicit environmental ethos.

# PROPERTY AND
# SELF-GOVERNMENT AS
# EDUCATIONAL INITIATIVES

*V. Deloria*

Indian students tend to look at education as a formal institutional experience. Core courses, graduation requirements, and electives when taken in sufficient quantities produce degrees and certificates. We are then authorized to perform certain functions in the adult world or become qualified to move on to the next level of educational complexity and attainment. In recent decades practical experience, the summer and semester internship and on-the-job training have begun to supplement formal academic studies, and the development of the paraprofessional in a number of areas offers a temporary resting place for those who are still uncertain of the attractiveness of the profession. Substantial education begins when the student, well trained in a profession, actually begins to perform professional tasks. At that point the accumulated experiences of applying abstract knowledge and principles to real-life problems and duties provides the final educational opportunity. We learn as we live and bring ideas and actions together.

In America the practical side of learning is taken for granted and in most instances is regarded as a higher activity than mere book learning. That is why we say that things are "academic" when we mean that they are essentially useless and have a certain degree of novelty. But the glorification of the self-made person, the worship of the school of hard knocks, and the demand that leadership have practical experience in identifiable fields mean that we cherish what we have been able to accumulate in the way of practical wisdom much more than we admire abstract thinking and precise intellectual analysis.

Students in higher education should become aware of the high premium that American society places on practical knowledge because it constitutes the hidden side of federal policy, and it is seen by most policy makers as a realistic alternative to formal academic training and services. Tracing federal efforts to provide academic training for American Indian children is not difficult. Educational experiments leap out of the pages of books and reports and are always described in highly emotional language. From the initial overture of English colonists in Virginia through the Meriam Report to the modern Kennedy Report, formal academic training is touted as the salvation of Indians and as the primary vehicle for assimilating Indians into the American mass society. But we have to dig carefully to see the other side of the coin, to see the multitude of times when Congress, frustrated at dealing with Indian problems, simply washed its hands of the whole thing and declared that Indians could learn by doing things for themselves. James Watt was not radically different from impatient bureaucrats of two centuries ago when it came to understanding the benefits of a practical education.

Looking at the history of federal policy, we can identify two areas in which Congress frequently refused to deal with complexities and instead advocated policies that would force Indians, whether they were prepared or not, to learn to live in American society using only their experiences as a guide. The two areas are the use and ownership of property and the efforts to establish a modicum of self-government. The guiding principle behind federal policy in these two areas is that Indians must be placed in a situation in which they have to confront and solve certain kinds of abstract and practical problems. Two entirely predictable results are produced by these policy changes. Indians sometimes succeed far beyond the expectations of Congress. If they are very successful it produces intense jealousy among neighboring whites and fear among federal bureaucrats, and then steps are taken to limit the potential of the program or it is terminated altogether. If the Indian adjustment does not make sense in the white person's terms, even if the Indians are pleased with the results, then the program is declared a failure. But the responsibility for the failure is placed on the Indian response, not on the rationality of the policy proposal in the first place.

We can easily illustrate the operation of these principles in the history of federal policy. First, however, we should examine the nature of practical education, as it is that practical aspect of things that non-Indian policy makers take for granted and upon which they rely even when all indications are that the direction policy takes will be a disaster. Practical education is the application of the abstract principle to conditions of real life. It is also the means of discovering principles for predicting future events based upon a vast reservoir of experiences of the same or similar events. While wholly academic knowledge is predictable, because we arrange it in a manner so that it will be predictable, knowledge gained through experience cannot be controlled. We learn both good and bad things from life, and consequently policy that naively believes that by creating conditions under which people learn through experience can have but one result—and that one a beneficial product—is not good policy. The flaw in the policy is that we cannot control the end product, and therefore we should not rely upon an abstract knowledge unless it has become such a part of community life that it is also practical knowledge. Let us now take a few examples from Indian history and see how practical knowledge or education has been a part of policy and what has happened to it.

## EXAMPLES FROM INDIAN HISTORY

In the early colonial days in Massachusetts, missionaries spent considerable time seeking converts among the tribes. People accepting Christianity were encouraged to adopt colonists' dress and habits, leave their families and communities, and take up residence in what came to be known as "Praying Towns." Sometimes, of course, whole families would convert, and occasionally bands and villages would make the transition to Christian life. It wasn't long before Massachusetts had a number of Praying Towns that were organized as regular townships with the same social and political institutions as other subdivisions of the Commonwealth. In making the transition—that is to say, in creating a town government, church, market, and all of the other institutions that New England life required—Indians learned both good and bad things from the whites around them. The result was that while some Indian towns functioned as well as their white neighbors, others did not. Shortcomings were blamed on the Indian character, and consequently Massachusetts introduced a trusteeship over the Indian towns. By the 1870s they had virtually eliminated self-government for the Indians of the state. Political status and property rights were essentially eliminated and the justification for divesting the Indians of these things was basically that they had learned the wrong lessons in the classroom of life.

The Removal Policy demonstrates even more clearly the relationship between practical education and political status and property rights. It was exceedingly difficult for federal representatives to deal with the tribes west of the Appalachians in the post–Revolutionary War period. So the tribes were told that if they adopted forms of government comparable to those used by the states and the federal government, it would facilitate the process of diplomacy and enable the federal government to provide services and protection for the tribes on a much more efficient basis. We can trace modifications of forms of government in almost every tribe who had dealings with the United States in the early decades of the nineteenth century. No changes are as clear as those adopted by the Cherokees, who sought to create a modern government and largely succeeded.

Presumably the success of the Cherokees in transforming their traditional ways into modern political institutions should have been sufficient to ensure them protection of their political status and property rights. However, the Cherokees were too successful. The local whites coveted the Cherokee lands, and eventually the state of Georgia simply moved its people in on those lands. When the problem reached the Supreme Court, it chose to define the Cherokees as a people in "tutelage," a people still on the verge of national existence but lacking the practical education and experience to make a successful transition. The Cherokees, and subsequently all Indian tribes thereafter, were described as "wards" of the government, as people who lacked sufficient education and maturity to make their own decisions.

As a result of the Removal Policy a large number of tribes were moved to Kansas and Oklahoma, the hope being that once beyond the reach of bad whites, the tribes could make a successful transition to civilized life. The Kansas Indians, learning through the school of hard knocks, became moderately successful in farming and adopted so many of the characteristics of their white neighbors that the state of Kansas believed they were no longer Indians and sought to tax them. The Supreme Court said no, and beginning with the Civil War and continuing a decade afterward, the Kansas tribes were pressured to sell their Kansas lands, most of which had been allotted, and move to Oklahoma where they would be given lands in communal status once again. The practical knowledge that they had acquired in Kansas was discounted by Congress because it had produced unexpected results. Thirty years later the tribes were again forced to take their lands in severalty so that they could once more learn from practical experience how to manage farming-sized tracts of land.

The pattern only becomes stronger as we approach contemporary times. The General Allotment Act was justified on the basis that the Indians needed to learn how to manage their property. In 1891, only four years after the passage of the act, it was amended to allow the secretary of the interior to manage allotments on behalf of the individuals. Presumably he was a more apt pupil—or perhaps needed the experience more. The Indian Reorganization Act of 1934 was touted as a great experiment in self-government. This in spite of the fact that the tribes had governed themselves adequately for thousands of years and had at least managed to preserve something of a homeland using the makeshift governments organized by the federal government in the 1870s and 1880s. Coincident with the allotment of lands and the support for self-government came changes in the federal government's educational programs.

Off-reservation boarding schools were being established in precisely the years that reservations were being allotted. During the Indian Reorganization Act, a loan fund was established to encourage Indians to attend college and advanced vocational and trade schools. By the time of the New Deal, educational programs both supported the existing trends in policy and forecast the future of policy direction.

In the 1950s termination became the dominant federal policy, and it was supposed to "free" Indians from unnecessary federal restrictions and allow them to use their property in the same manner as other American citizens. No sane capitalist, however, would have sold a large virgin standing forest as the Klamaths were forced to do, and no white businessperson would have agreed to use his or her sawmill as the sole tax base for a county as the Menominees were required to do. Additionally, and here is where the theory of termination was revealed as totally bankrupt, both the Klamaths and Menominees were placed under private trustees so that the practical experience they were supposed to receive from termination became, once again, an education that their trustees enjoyed to the detriment of the tribes.

Termination of the various tribes coincided with the push to relocate individual Indians and their families to western and midwestern urban centers. Relocation and vocational training were the major emphases of the federal government until the mid-1960s, when, because the program was such an embarrassment to the federal government, it was retitled "Employment Assistance" and relegated to a minor item in the Bureau of Indian Affairs' budget. In terms of both formal academic and the more practical vocational education, the 1950s demonstrated that an intimate link existed between what was offered to Indians in the way of educational programs and desperate attempts by Congress to make the natural resources of the reservation lands available to white Americans and to reduce tribal government to nearly an advisory capacity.

RECENT EVENTS AND PROGRAMS

The last four decades are very interesting when examined in this larger historical pattern. Events and programs have moved so fast that there is no longer a time lag between manipulation of property and tribal status and the promulgation of additional educational programs. Indian tribes were supposed to absorb simultaneously the policy of self-determination, rapid development of reservation lands, and rapid changes in educational programs. The result was a rare intersection in which educational programs were narrowed to produce administrators and managers, with a smattering of science and professional fields factored in. Among the problems created in this massive change were the shifting reservoir of resources available to the tribes to develop programs, the educational requirements necessary to operate programs, and the absence of a time lag between the conception and operation of programs.

Many economic development programs were funded under the guise of vocational training; other economic programs had to be recast as vocational training because of a lack of Indian experience in certain fields. Eligibility for employment in some programs depended wholly on academic achievements, and Indians with degrees in forestry and other hard sciences often found themselves operating educational programs or trying to administer complicated umbrella development programs. Evaluations of programs funded with federal dollars often began at about the same time that the programs themselves started, making it impossible to judge what effects the program actually would have on the reservations. Not only were conditions extremely confusing, but under Ronald Reagan, George Bush, and Bill Clinton, federal funding was reduced drastically, making it imperative that Indian tribes find alternative sources of funding for economic development, tribal government, and education. As we begin the new century, many tribes can be described as existing at ground zero, reduced to providing the very minimal programs their communities need to exist.

Although many tribal leaders take a pessimistic view of the present situation, when we see modern conditions in a historical perspective we can see that there is reason for considerable optimism. It is no longer possible for Congress to announce a new program of changing the status of tribal governments or tribal property with the naive hope that through practical education Indians will be able to accomplish some nebulous goal of assimilating into American society. Indeed, the new federalism, even if it is to remain but an unfounded slogan, clearly shows that the tendency of Congress is to devise new methods whereby Indians can define their paths for the future. Blithe views of the efficacy of private property no longer prevail, and even though recent Supreme Court decisions have tended to limit the scope of tribal powers, the legislative trend is clearly to vest more programs, powers, and responsibilities in tribal governments.

## THE MODERN EDUCATIONAL EXPERIENCE

What is the relevance of connecting practical education, as seen in policy changes of the past, with modern educational problems? And what further insights can be gained by today's college-age Indian students in viewing, in this much longer historical perspective, the educational programs in which they are engaged? What does the relationship of practical, ill-conceived education and formal academic training have to tell us about the immediate prospects of jobs for graduating Indian students? These questions and many others now surround the modern educational experience. Taken together they suggest that we look at professional education in an entirely different manner. The professional education, particularly that education in the hard sciences and computers, has basically replaced practical education because the lack of lag time between when a policy is initiated and when it is supposed to be operating has been reduced to practically zero. We need expertise in order to consider programs. For the first time in Indian history we can place practical, on-the-job training after the authorization of policy changes.

Indians with professional expertise must now be prepared to offer their tribes predictive scenarios based upon their professional training. The degree to which an Indian professional can succeed with any tribal program will be measured by the number of possible scenarios with which he or she presents the tribe. It will then be the task of the tribe to choose among possible competing scenarios. Tribes will have to choose from alternatives based upon their analysis of existing resources and level of education. Even more important, however, is that much of modern scientific thought, particularly that dealing with the environment, closely parallels traditional perspectives on how lands, peoples, and resources should be used. The absence of a time lag between articulation of policy and the mustering of resources to carry it out suggests that for the first time in history there can and must be Indian input into program planning.

Some planners may argue that there has always been Indian input in reservation development plans, but this argument is difficult to sustain. While the Bureau of Indian Affairs was busy expanding the number of Indian college students during the early 1960s, Congress was significantly expanding the potential for tribes to lease their lands for ninety-nine years, and the bureau was pressuring tribes to develop massive programs to exploit natural resources of the reservations. Although the gap between professionally trained Indians and tribal activities was lessening during this period, it was certainly not in any sense being coordinated in order to produce maximum or even any sensible results. The uranium mining and strip-mining programs of the 1960s and 1970s probably could not occur today on many Indian reservations because professional expertise has caught up to or is only slightly behind proposed projects.

Indian students working with tribal development programs will notice a slight but important shift in emphasis in tribal perspectives. They will no longer be expected to provide direction for tribal programs, but they will be expected to provide a significant amount of technical information so that tribal councils can make proper decisions. We can characterize modern Indian students as fulfilling the function of scouts in the old hunting culture. They did not direct tribal activities as much as they provided information upon which the community could act. Indian education from colonial days until very recently was conceived as producing individuals who could and would lead their people into American society's economic mainstream. While many of today's programs are still phrased in those terms, they are not the conditions under which Indian professionals will be helpful to their tribes in the future.

We can learn an additional important lesson from this longer perspective on practical education. Any future effort by Congress to manipulate either the use of reservation natural resources or the political status of tribes will almost certainly produce a massive reaction in the field of education. Perhaps the newer studies of Indian education will be triggered by the rapid expansion of gambling activities on reservations or by the drastic budget cuts of recent years. What we must always remember is that education does not stand alone among other Indian and congressional activities. It is always an intimate part of policy considerations, and educated Indians must at all times be aware of events taking place in noneducational fields.

The relationship between education and lands and political status is an area of cultural conflict that has not been resolved in this half millennium of contact between Indians and other peoples. All education, formal academic education and practical educational learning experiences, exists in the gulf between Indians and other peoples and their perspectives on the nature of the world. There would be no use for formal education if worldviews were more similar. But if the white majority has chosen education as the field in which the difference in cultural perspective must be worked out, then Indians have to be particularly alert as to the nature of education and what non-Indians seek to accomplish with it. Whatever Indians are asked to do must be done from within the traditional Indian perspective, from a critical examination of the nature of the task, and with the understanding that professional expertise is but a specific body of knowledge existing within the gulf between the two cultures.

Indian students must therefore look at their professional education not simply from its set of coherent internal logics that make the professional field unique but also from two additional perspectives. How does what we receive in our educational experience impact the preservation and sensible use of our lands, and how does it affect the continuing existence of our tribes? These questions must always be asked during the educational years of training. There will not often be good answers because of the difficulty in applying abstract information to existing human communities. Nevertheless, Indian students will find a much more rewarding educational experience if they raise these questions in every educational context in which they find themselves.

# PRACTICAL PROFESSIONAL
# INDIGENOUS EDUCATION

*D. Wildcat*

Deloria raises a number of issues that should be considered by Indian students and teachers alike if we are to advance tribal interests through education in general, and specifically "professional" education. Three issues I want to expand on are as follows. First, what kind of institution can create professionals with indigenous values and beliefs? Second, how can we use the disappearance "of a lag time between articulation of policy and the mustering of resources to carry it out" to the advantage of education and self-determination? And third, given what I will call the "damned if you do and damned if you don't" consequence of federal educational initiatives, how do you ensure that the goals or ends of tribal initiatives are practical?

PRACTICAL INDIGENOUS PROFESSIONALS

What kind of professionals do we need in "Indian Country?" The necessary condition is that they receive the requisite technical knowledge, skills, and abilities to advise Indian communities on an array of possible solutions and scenarios to address specific problems/issues. However, this is not a sufficient condition to meet the tribal needs of culturally distinct indigenous peoples. Any tribal councilperson or politically engaged tribal member can testify to the fact that often when non-Indian professionals are hired to do things for tribes, the clash in underlying worldviews—that is, indigenous-versus-Western conflict—makes accomplishment of tribal goals difficult, if not impossible.

The problem of professional expertise in institutions of higher education is that "expertise" is thought of as culture-free or value-neutral. It is true that most American Indian students feel they are "caught between two cultures" throughout their technical and professional education, but I would argue that professional and technical education in fact is not "a specific body of knowledge existing within the gulf between two cultures." Rather, professional education and the resulting "expertise" are implicitly value-laden and reflective of the schizophrenic metaphysics of Western society.

We can fairly easily describe the attributes we want American Indian professionals to have and identify the questions we hope they will keep foremost in their minds. Also, there can be little doubt that students in science, engineering, and business programs often feel caught between two cultures. I have seen students confront these professional programs with considerable disorientation. In fact, there is no greater ex post facto demonstration of the existence of indigenous cultures than the dominant Western culture in America; nor is there a better demonstration of the schizophrenic nature of the world that modern Western institutions, and especially educational institutions, create and advocate. According to one dictionary, *schizophrenia* is defined as "a psychotic disorder characterized by loss of contact with environment and by disintegration of personality." An introduction into most American institutions of higher education should predictably result in disorientation to any person who understands their personality as emergent from a specific environment or *place*.

How do we address this profound experiential disorientation? I suggest we create our own indigenous institutions to prepare American Indian professionals. Some will say we have those institutions, we have the tribal colleges. Yes, we do, and they are often working miracles in spite of the limited resources they possess. But the overhead costs—equipment, supplies, facilities, and so on—of operating science and engineering programs are much higher than for liberal arts programs. Also, given the size of reservation populations served by the tribal colleges and the already limited resources for existing programs, it is simply unfeasible for each tribal college to implement and develop programs resulting in their own science/engineering degrees. Typically this leaves two options to tribes and/or their colleges: (1) working with majority institutions (state universities) to create bridge programs, Two Plus Two or Two Plus Three programs that address the "academic" needs of Indian students who will matriculate to the majority institution to acquire their degree by completing coursework they cannot get at the tribal college, or (2) sending their students to colleges and universities with support programs to assist American Indian students in successful matriculation to majority institutions.

Both options are inadequate, for they fail to confront in a meaningful manner the root of the struggle Indian students face. Deloria, maybe more than any other scholar living today, has positioned the questions about self-determination and sovereignty in the most radical context possible: the real world or, if you want a technical description, a phenomenological critical realism.

Deloria is correct to refer to a disorientation resulting from the conflict between cultures, not worlds; we must avoid the error of talking about life in two different worlds or realities. Sorry, postmodernist and critical deconstructionist, but as I read Deloria, I find his point for almost four decades has been to suggest in the broadest sense that questions about our indigenous education, and for that matter the future of humanity itself, revolve precisely around who we are and how we choose to live in the world. We American Indians have done ourselves a great disservice by speaking of "living in two worlds"—the Western or dominant American culture and our own tribal indigenous cultures.

The needs that both typical options address are almost exclusively academic or intellectual. Do not misunderstand my point. Reasoning skills and intellectual needs are real, what I called the necessary condition for indigenous professionalization, but they are insufficient in and of themselves and possibly counterproductive in creating professionals with a complex integrated or holistic indigenous understanding of our lives in the world. The above options fail to address the question of how scientific and technical knowledge are understood as a part of a large living system of which we human beings are but one small part.

The problem with the typical options Indian students must choose from is that, as usual, that they miss the point—the big picture. At the University of Kansas Red Power Conference in the fall of 2000, Ladonna Harris made the point emphatically: "We do not live in two worlds. If you try to do that you will be schizophrenic." We are surrounded by a society of metaphysical schizophrenics: people who do not see the phenomenal world for what it is—a living, complex reality with multiple dimensions. A good number of these metaphysical schizophrenics are scientists and engineers who have, with considerable harm to their person (or personality) as human beings, convinced themselves that their feelings or emotions have no place in their objective science. This is the metaphysics of the world writ large.

AN INDIGENOUS INSTITUTE OF
SCIENCE AND TECHNOLOGY IN CULTURE

I would propose American Indian leaders, students, and professionals get together to examine practical consideration of how American Indians and Alaska Natives might create our own MIT—Massachusetts Institute of Technology. We can call it whatever we like, but the goal would be practical indigenous professionalism: technology with an indigenous personality.

I expect all kinds of objections. Some will fear an institute of pan-Indian culture and technology, others will worry about funding and control, and still others may suggest technical issues are distinct from cultural questions. Nevertheless, the reality in Indian country today is most of our tribes are depending—no, dependent —on the advice of non-Indian scientists and engineers who work with conceptual blind spots relative to our indigenous worldviews.

We desperately need indigenous scientists and engineers, but not in the mold of those produced by the dominant educational institutions of the United States. Can we create our own indigenous institutes of science and technology in culture? I think a cursory look at the moneymaking activities among some tribes suggests the answer is yes. But will we? This remains to be seen, but I hope so. It would require a strategic long-term, multi- or intertribal effort for an institution the likes of which has never been seen. Given the never-ending rounds of seminars for strategic planning, empowerment, and creative problem solving that foundations and organizations are constantly holding in Indian country, I have no doubt about our ability to create a plan.

The challenge, and opportunity, really, is to develop a network of indigenous philanthropy, something that only recently has it made sense to talk about, which can ensure a substantial period of infrastructure building. The cost will be high in dollars; however, the cost of not creating indigenous institutions to our peoples and the places where we live will be exponentially higher.

Sobering is the only way I can describe my reaction after attending two environmental justice conferences recently. If one contemplates the enormity of the problems facing rural and urban minority communities, including those of indigenous peoples, in the United States and throughout the world, one certainly comes away sobered. But hopefully one is reinvigorated too, with a dedication to finding creative ways to solve environmental problems we human beings have produced—not intentionally, but by virtue of a relatively abstract universal worldview where first, humans are the measure of all things, and second, an Aristotelian compartmentalizing and categorizing of human experience prejudices exploration of human experience itself.

Basic research, technology transfer, reliable information, bioremediation (ecology-based as opposed to genetics-oriented) technologies, and ultimately community service—all of these can be accomplished by creating an institution that prepares and provides indigenized professional education: practices supportive of cultural diversity emergent out of the diverse geographies and ecologies of the places we call home. We have a long history of being given bad advice, and we are paying the price today. If we are going to make mistakes—and we will—let them be our mistakes. Much of the technology we see being used today has been developed to address environmental cleanup activities; our actions are essentially reactive in character.

On a recent visit to a sister institution, something struck me as we watched the demonstration of a state-of-the-art technology developed to address accidents involving the release of deadly airborne chemicals. Much of what scientist, engineers, and businesspeople work on today is cleanup. My colleague and Potawatomi ecologist George Godfrey has talked often about the creation of a cadre of American Indian environmental scientists and engineers who would achieve success and a status comparable to the highly praised American Indian "smoke-jumpers" in the U.S. Forest Service.

## INDIGENIZING PROFESSIONAL INTERNSHIPS

We have plenty of environmental "fires" to put out in our communities, and we need well-trained American Indian professionals to do so. Here then is precisely the place where we use the disappearance of lag time between policy development and mustering of resources to realize policy goals to the advantage of practical indigenous professionalism. Our young scientists, engineers, and entrepreneurs would serve required yearlong internships in communities, working on problems people are facing. This will not be easy; the level of coordination and direction from professionals will be time-intensive. However, the much ballyhooed technology of the Internet and World Wide Web could actually serve to have students working on problems in real places, in communities, where beliefs, values, and practices count for something. This experiential learning will accomplish what case studies or "virtual" realities can merely suggest: the world is more complex than our models and neat conceptual categories lead us to believe.

Community service ought to be expected, and I can think of no better service than holistic learning experiences in which students learn that the best solution to a problem will be power-, place-, and personality-specific. The irony in doing so is that the experience itself overcomes the greatest obstacle to the biological, environmental (ecological), and cultural diversity on the planet: an abstract system of analytical education that rivals the heights of medieval scholastic education. In fact, serious consideration ought to be given to reinstituting community service (something that occurs naturally in nonmodern societies) through all the grades of education. Such activities would indeed be practical and, with a little thought to who we are as tribal peoples, indigenizing.

We can take advantage of the disappearing "time lag between the conception and operation of programs" by situating professional programs in our communities. It is a disservice to everyone to continue to think "experts" go off to school somewhere and then come back with the all the answers. Now, everyone will say, we all know that, the real world just does not work that way. Okay, then why do we continue to "educate" in exactly that manner? If we create professional internships for scientists, engineers, and business professionals, the world they live in would engender practical, creative insights into the largely artificial disciplinary boxes our institutions of higher education perpetuate.

The knowledge human beings all over this planet once possessed was of places; modern technologies have certainly reduced the "time constraints" of distance. But what time is it? It depends on where you are. Once we disabuse ourselves of the abstract and essentially linear universal notion of world historical time, as Deloria critiqued three decades ago in "Thinking in Time and Space" in *God Is Red*, we may indeed reexamine our histories in a light much different than the current progress-of-civilization model. In our human lifetimes (appointment books, clocks, schedules, and calendars) we have disconnected ourselves from natural histories much larger than ourselves and with the aid technology forgotten what geographies and natural environments have to give us: unique cultural identities in the place of an increasingly homogenized global consumer identity. Western civilization, as the vanguard of globalization, seems to have forgotten this valuable gift that indigenous cultures have not.

## No Longer "Damned" Up

Deloria has put his finger on the problem with federal Indian initiatives in general. It matters little whether the issues were oriented toward property, self-government, or education, as the cultural gulf between the majority of Americans and American Indians was so great that success, even if assessed by essentially Western measures, and failure, which was always seen in the eyes of federal lawmakers as an issue of *not* measuring up, inevitably meant we were, colloquially speaking, "damned if we do and damned if we don't."

The modest but meaningful gains that our indigenous nations have made in self-determination mean that we have choices our ancestors did not. As my friend and colleague Michael Yellowbird frames the situation: although we have moved from a colonial situation, the question remains, are we intellectually colonized, have our worldviews, so to speak, been colonized? Our children today and grandchildren tomorrow will soon find out.

Can we escape the "damned if we do and damned if we don't" maxim? Only if we set our own goals by our own set of measures, which is much easier said than done. We have been subject to so many experiments, pilot programs, and policy initiatives that the first obstacle is to get over a knee-jerk aversion to sitting down to identify goals and objectives, and discussing ways to meet them. We can do it, but long years of experience taught us that "our" goals inevitably meant their goals. Consequently, many of us are immediately suspicious the moment discussion of such things comes up.

An even more fundamental problem is that we have been struggling for existence itself for so long that too many of us have had little time to explore precisely what are our particular tribe's measures of success. Fortunately, we have elders who retain the wisdom and who have much to teach, although not necessarily through pedagogy but through living. We also have large numbers of indigenous professionals and scholars who know what was missing in their formal education. We have allies as we enter the twenty-first century—increasing numbers of young people and more than a few of their teachers who are struggling to find more meaningful ways of learning and living.

One measure of indigenous success, I believe, would be a generation of professionals who understand the world as not revolving around humankind, but rather humankind as surrounded by relatives, including other-than-human persons. Oren Lyons, Onadoga elder, remarked at the twenty-fifth anniversary of Earth Day that the difference between American Indian and Western views of nature is that while European immigrants looked at nature and saw resources, we looked around and saw relatives. Indigenous professionals who live in the world with relatives and focus on relations would be very different than professionals who study resources (objects) and focus on control. This would be progress, not as it is typically thought of today, but as a sign that a return to questions about living, as opposed to struggling for existence, is still possible and more crucially necessary.

# HIGHER EDUCATION AND
# SELF-DETERMINATION

*V. Deloria*

During the 1950s Congress authorized a program of rapid termination of federal trust responsibilities for American Indians. The policy was ill-conceived, seeking to reduce federal expenditures that were minimal, and badly executed, allowing private banks to exercise a restrictive supervision over the assets of tribes who lost their federal eligibility. Virtually no development of tribal assets occurred during this period, and educational programs were generally oriented toward vocational training and relocation of Indian families to designated urban areas. With the New Frontier and the Great Society programs came a radical redirection of Indian programs. Economic development was stressed and the federal government began to provide scholarship funds for Indians in higher education.

We have been living in the era of self-determination since about 1966, and, although appropriations suffered immensely during the Reagan and older Bush years, the trend of policy has firmly supported preserving tribal life and enhancing the powers of tribal self-government. The two major thrusts of federal policy from the very beginning have been the education of the next generation of Indians in the ways of the white people and the exploitation and/or development of the reservation resources. Today the government seems intent on stressing the economic aspect of Indian life to the detriment of its educational component, a policy exceedingly shortsighted in view of the continuing economic crisis of the United States and the limited resources Indian reservations actually contain.

Self-determination grew like a weed over the past four decades, and it never was clearly defined at the onset of the era. It was a concept that originally surfaced in international relations to describe the desire of formerly colonized peoples to break free from their European oppressors and take control over their own lives. These peoples were, for the most part, geographically distinct and distant from their former colonial masters, and consequently independence, while painful, seemed more logical because the connections established by colonizing powers seemed and were wholly artificial. Indian tribes, with the possible exception of western and north-slope Alaskan villages, have always been viewed as internal to the United States and hence part of its domestic problems. That the Supreme Court has continually characterized Indian tribes as foreign to the United States in cultural and political traditions is difficult for most people to understand, so they make little effort to do so and prefer to consider Indians as simply another racial minority, albeit one with considerably fascinating habits.

Self-determination inevitably had to take on a different meaning when applied to Indian tribes and reservations. And as the original goal of the Kennedy and Johnson administrations was to delay termination of federal services until such time as tribes achieved some measure of economic parity with their white neighbors, self-determination in the Indian context basically has meant that Indians can administer their own programs in lieu of federal bureaucrats. Education was conceived as the handmaiden of development. One need only look at the fields in which Title IV fellowships are being given to understand that federal higher education programs were meant to train a generation of people who could function as low-level bureaucrats in drastically underfunded programs—programs intended only to keep Indians active and fearful of losing their extra federal funding.

Two major emphases characterized Indian economic development. Tribes were encouraged to allow major American corporations to control their energy resources in exchange for a few token jobs and a small income. Employment programs were designed to provide temporary wage labor in fringe industries that were themselves in danger of disappearing. Some wage industries, such as the moccasin factory at Pine Ridge, attempted to exploit the public stereotypes of Indians, and others, such as recreational ventures, placed the Indian workers in the permanent status of servants to a rich non-Indian clientele. Administration and management have thus become the favorite programs of the federal government and private foundations, the belief being that Indians feel more comfortable in performing menial jobs or watching their forests and coal reserves being exhausted if some token Indians are involved.

Unfortunately, administration and management have never been areas in which Indians have excelled. These types of jobs require that people be viewed as objects and that masses of people be moved and manipulated at will in order that programs achieve maximum efficiency. This kind of attitude and behavior is the antithesis of Indians' ways as is the fact that management and administration are always dressed up in "people" language to make them more palatable. Many Indians did not realize that the programs they were administering were designed to manipulate people, and they unintentionally transformed administrative procedures to fit Indian expectations. The result was that program efficiency declined, and some programs fell apart even while an increasing number of people were being served. Many programs considered as failures from the non-Indian perspective have been outstanding successes when considered from the Indian side of the ledger, even if they have given bureaucrats ulcers.

Indian education of the past four decades has done more than train Indian program chiefs, however. While Indians have been penetrating the institutions of higher learning, the substance and procedures of these institutions have also been affecting Indians. Indians have found even the most sophisticated academic disciplines and professional schools woefully inadequate. This is because the fragmentation of knowledge that is represented by today's modern university does not allow for a complete understanding of a problem or of a phenomenon. Every professor and professional must qualify his or her statements on reality and truth with the admonition that their observations are being made from a legal, political, sociological, anthropological, or other perspective. These statements then are true if confined to the specific discipline and methodology by which they are formed. That they represent little else may escape the professor or professional, but it does not escape the Indian student, who often dismisses theory, doctrine, or interpretation when it does not ring true to his or her experience.

The revolt against social sciences is not simply a few Indian activists criticizing anthropologists and the suspicion with which Indians in science and engineering view theories in their fields. Rather, the problem is the credibility and applicability of Western knowledge in the Indian context. The objections are easily understood. Western technology largely depletes resources or substitutes a monocultural approach to a complex natural system. We tend to hide this fact by talking about production rather than extraction, but this linguistic acrobatics is not sufficient to escape Indian critique. Social science in the Western context describes human behavior in such restrictive terminology that it really describes very little except the methodology acceptable to the present generation of academics and researchers. While an increasing number of Indian students are mastering the language and theoretical frameworks of Western knowledge, there remain the feelings of incompleteness and inadequacy about what has been learned.

More importantly, whatever information is obtained in higher education must, in the Indian context, have some direct bearing on human individual and communal experience. In contrast, in the non-Indian context the knowledge must simply provide a means of identification of the experience or phenomenon. It helps to deal with specific examples to illustrate the point. A Western observer faced with the question of how and why certain species of birds make their nests is liable to conclude that it is "instinct." And this identification of course tells us nothing whatsoever, but it does foreclose further inquiry because a question has been answered.

In the Indian context the answer would involve a highly complicated description of the personality of the bird species, be it eagle, meadowlark, or sparrow; and the observed behavior of the bird would provide information on time of year, weather, absence or presence of related plants and animals, and perhaps even some indication of the age and experience of the particular bird. In this comparison Indian knowledge provides a predictive context in which certain prophetic statements can be made. Western science, for all its insistence on reproduction of behavior and test conditions and predictability of future activities, provides us with very little that is useful.

Indian knowledge is designed to make statements that adequately describe the experience or phenomenon. That is to say, they include everything that is known about the experience even if no firm conclusions are reached. There are many instances in the oral traditions of the tribe in which, after reviewing everything that is known about a certain thing, the storyteller simply states that what he or she has said was passed down by elders or that he or she marveled at the phenomenon and was unable to explain it further. It is permissible within the Indian context to admit that something mysterious remains after all is said and done. Western science seems incapable of admitting that anything mysterious can exist or that any kind of behavior or experience can remain outside its ability to explain. Often in the Western context the answer is derived by the process of elimination. Thus with the theory of evolution, it is accepted primarily because other explanations are not popular or are distasteful.

Western engineering presents a special case. Its validity depends primarily on its ability to force nature to perform certain tasks that we believe are useful to human beings. Its knowledge derives from physical experiments, and more recently on complicated mathematical formulas that predict certain kinds of phenomena if certain kinds of things are done under conditions controlled by human beings. There is no question that if engineers restrict our understanding of the world to particular things we want to do, and set up the conditions under which they must occur, the results are spectacular. But does the engineer really understand nature or the natural world? Does he or she not simply force natural entities to do specific tasks and provide a theoretical explanation for what has happened? In forcing nature to behave in certain controlled ways, have we not set in motion other forces that nature must make manifest so that the demands of the experiment can be met?

Today there is no question that our society is approaching the brink of an ecological meltdown. We have identified certain aspects of our forceful interferences with nature and have come to believe these things to be the cause of the deterioration we have observed. We have no way of knowing how things relate to deterioration because our context is too small. Would the widespread use of electricity, for example, have anything to do with the ozone problem? Does increased radiation have anything to do with the rapid disappearance of amphibians around the world? Is cancer a function of crowding people together, or is AIDS a function of chemically treated foods and chemical disposal into domestic water supplies? When we begin to ask questions that try to bring byproducts of our technology into new combinations so that we can test effects and do further investigations, we are virtually helpless because we have no good context within which to ask the questions that should be asked. In this society, we must spend immense amounts of time and energy simply identifying the proper questions.

When Indian students take all of the knowledge received in colleges and universities, along with certifications for professional work and perhaps even for managerial activities, they are led to believe that Indians are prepared to exercise self-determination because educated Indians are now able to begin to compete with the non-Indian world for funds, resources, and rights. But we must ask ourselves, where is the self-determination? What is it that we Indians as selves and communities are determining? We will find that we are basically agreeing to model our lives, values, and experiences along non-Indian lines. Now, the argument can be made that because we are geographically within the United States, we must conform to its values, procedures, and institutions. At least we must do so if we are to measure success according to the same standards and criteria. And all of our education informs us that these standards are nationally acceptable and may indeed even be universal throughout the cosmos.

It is increasingly apparent, however, that the myths of Western civilization are also the cause of its rapid degeneration, so that it is hazardous to measure ourselves according to those standards. As a nation we no longer produce wealth as much as we borrow from the future. If an individual really wants to make money he or she would do better to master complicated tax laws than to start a new business. Professors stand more chance of getting their ideas accepted if they are immensely popular with their peers than if they actually have something to contribute. The possible existence of a Supreme Being is a great embarrassment to religious people. Poor people are or should be incubators and organ donors for rich people. Wisdom consists of frequent appearances on television shows. Athletes need not be skillful, but they must win regardless of the circumstances. Any form of change in any other country can be regarded as a threat to the United States—and of course all forms of progressive change within the United States are perceived as threats to its security. It is exceedingly difficult to distinguish between American moral values and bumper sticker slogans.

The practical reality of these insights provides both the criteria for public success and the uncomfortable feeling among educated Indians that something is missing. Most Indians do not see themselves and their relatives within the popular American truisms, and they are greatly embarrassed when other people force them to acknowledge that these criteria really are accepted by a majority of Americans. Minimally, Western mythology describes a society that is not even polite. That is the key to understanding how to transcend the attitudes and perspectives of non-Indian education, so that Indians can determine for themselves and by themselves what they want to be, even if they are wholly within the confines of American society.

When we talk of the old days and old ways, we frequently give special emphasis to the manner in which people treated each other, the sense of propriety, gentility, and confidence that the elders had. Being polite springs primarily from a sense of confidence in one's self and one's knowledge about the world. Indian narration of knowledge about the world fell into a particular format, and out of a plenitude of data, the speaker would choose the set of facts most pertinent to the explanation. He or she would formulate the story so that it ended on a proper note—*oh han* as the Sioux say. Now, a person cannot bring a teaching to a close, invoke the right response in the listener so that the information is taken seriously, and have some impact without closing off the discussion on a proper note. Real knowledge creates politeness in the personality, and one can see this trait in many wise non-Indians. It is, in fact, their foremost personality trait.

In the past four decades, while the movement for self-determination was proceeding, we have witnessed a drastic decline in politeness and civility in Indian communities. Indian meetings are many times difficult to attend because they consist of little more than people clamoring for attention and people busy impressing each other. The outstanding characteristic of Indian students today is the emergence of politeness as a personality trait. Science and engineering students more than others now seem to possess this most precious of all the old traditional personality traits. Here we may have an indication that the current generation of Indian youth is moving beyond the boundaries established for non-Indian self-determination, and now this generation stands ready to bring something entirely new to the process of applying Western scientific knowledge to Indian problems.

If this observation is correct, then we will witness some very unusual things happening in Indian communities in the future. Indians who are now working at the professional level, particularly in science and engineering, will work their way through corporate and academic institutions and begin appearing as independent consultants and owners of small, technologically oriented businesses working in ecological restoration and conservation areas. Research institutes headed by Indians will begin to appear on certain college and university campuses doing complex research projects. Almost all of this first generation of Indians will be active in traditional religious practices, even though many of them will be living away from their reservations. One or two of these people will write extremely sophisticated papers and books that will be highly regarded in their professions.

Indian students in colleges and universities will begin to combine majors, putting together unlikely and unpredictable fields. They will have some degree of difficulty doing so because of the departments' inability to reconcile the students' interest within traditional Western disciplinary relationships. An increasing number of Indian students will choose very specific new majors that represent non-Indian efforts to do interdisciplinary work and that are almost entirely outside the fields being chosen by present Indian students. Indian graduate students will be doing very sophisticated dissertations, and in hard sciences, highly innovative research projects.

Indian community colleges will begin to show an increasing non-Indian enrollment, some people being nonresidents who come to these schools specifically to study with certain tribal elders. The number of four-year community colleges will dramatically increase, and community colleges themselves will begin to appear on the national scene in scholarly conferences and meetings. Most of the larger community colleges will have their own publishing and TV production programs, and some of them will be producing programs for national educational television. Some faculty at reservation community colleges will begin thriving consultant businesses because state and private universities far from the reservation will want to establish working relationships with the tribes. Community colleges will play an increasingly influential role in tribal economic and political problems and programs.

Tribal governments will develop new ways to organize the reservation communities and will develop specific programs for a wide variety of land uses. Tribal governments will have a considerably larger role in determining high school curricula, and some reservation high schools will have entirely new formats for study and graduation. Formal and informal networks of elders will begin to resolve some of the reservation problems, radically changing the kinds of topics that tribal councils are asked to handle. New and smaller communities will be built in different parts of the reservation, eliminating the concentrations at agency towns and having new kinds of local governing powers. Self-determination will not be an issue because people will be doing it in forms that even they will not recognize.

Although it appears easy to make vague predictions concerning the future of Indians and education, none of these ideas is an ad hoc concept. Rather, everything flows from the original idea of education acting as the motivational force in self-determination. The policy makers four decades ago *assumed* education would radically change Indian young people while also assuming that they would hold, as a constant, the value of returning to their tribes to take the lead in development projects. Higher education really was thought to be higher than the knowledge and experiences that Indians brought from their homes and communities. Higher education might have been more complicated, but it was too departmentalized, and consequently the chinks in the armor were all too apparent and left most Indian students with a feeling of having an incomplete knowledge. Unable to bring academic knowledge to its proper unity, more and more students are now supplementing the shortcoming of Western thought by placing it in the context of their own tribal traditions.

Once the process of supplementation began, it would naturally follow that individuals would begin to compare specific items of Western knowledge with similar beliefs derived wholly from the traditions of their tribes. We see this process now emerging as an identifiable intellectual position of this generation of Indians. It will take a considerable period of time for a new theoretical posture to be developed by this generation, but some individuals are well on their way to doing so. As a new perspective is formed, individual Indians who have moved completely through the institutional structures will take all conceptions of Indians beyond the ability of Western ideas to compete, and this conceptual shift will focus attention on the cultural knowledge of the community colleges. Once community colleges articulate a new conception of what it means to be an Indian and an Indian community, the rest of the shift is apparent and predictable.

In a previous essay I discussed the fact that much of American education is really just training and indoctrination into the Western view of the world. Basically this view is held together by the sincerity of its followers. It does not have an internal consistency of its own except in general methodological patterns whereby information is classified. Indians, over the long run, are exceedingly hard to train because they get easily bored with the routine of things. Once they have understood and mastered a task it seems like a waste of time to simply repeat an activity. So for an increasing number of Indians the training received at institutions of higher learning only raises fundamental questions that are never answered to their satisfaction.

We can visualize the effects of education on Indians as follows. Non-Indians live within a worldview that separates and isolates and mistakes labeling and identification for knowledge. Indians were presumed to be within this condition except they were slower on the uptake and not nearly as bright as non-Indians. In truth Indians were completely outside the system and within their own worldview. Initiating an accelerated educational system for Indians was intended to bring Indians up to the parity of middle-class non-Indians. In fact, this system has pulled Indians into the Western worldview, and some of the brighter ones are now emerging on the other side, having transversed the Western body of knowledge completely. Once this path has been established, it is almost a certainty that the rest of the Indian community will walk right on through the Western worldview and emerge on the other side also. And it is imperative that we do so. Only in that way can we transcend the half millennium of culture shock brought about by the confrontation with Western civilization. When we leave the culture shock behind we will be masters of our own fate again and able to determine for ourselves what kind of lives we will lead.

# The Question
# of Self-Determination

*D. Wildcat*

WHAT IS SELF-DETERMINATION?

Locating education within the framework of self-determination is critical, for Deloria is asking the question seldom asked: "What do we, indigenous peoples of the Americas, mean by self-determination?" If we accept the standards and criteria of mainstream education in America and its fundamental Western claim of universal and objective applicability to the world and the cosmos itself, then, whether we are aware of it or not, we have accepted the metaphysical assumptions and premises that lead to a good number of problems Western society seems unable to address. American Indians are now in the position to, as Deloria states, "compete with the non-Indian world for funds, resources, and rights," and he continues, "We must ask ourselves, where is the self-determination? What is it that we as selves and communities are determining? We will find that we are basically agreeing to model our lives, values, and experiences along non-Indian lines."

I think many of our ancestors and present elders would see good and bad in the proposition that we culturally conform to the dominant values, procedures, and institutions of the United States. But before we grab hold of the obvious improvement in terms of physical and material comforts, we must assess our experience in the big picture of life. Once we acknowledge this larger, more complex context, we will see that the issues are not about what is practical in some normative cultural context, but about the nature of reality itself.

It is not surprising that in modern American society economic initiatives inevitably overshadow education programs. Education as an institution reflects the values of the larger society, and the only thing historically distinguishing so-called Indian education from mainstream education is the direct and blatant regimen in which culture was instilled. Today the notion that educational "progress" is identified with economic measures is so widely accepted that the business of education has become business. Many neoliberal economists even argue that the marketplace will democratize backward, nondemocratic peoples and instill in them the values of liberty and justice for all—making individuals, in the words of Milton Freidman, "free to choose," or more correctly, as friend and sociologist Dean Braa used to say, "free to lose." Our challenge as we enter the twenty-first century is to ensure that as we focus on gains, we do not forget about what we might lose as indigenous peoples in undertaking certain activities.

## SELF-DETERMINATION IN THE ABSTRACT

The question "What is self-determination?" is the easiest question in the world to answer in the abstract, and, for the most part, that is precisely how it has been answered. In the abstract we can say self-determination is when one freely chooses to act or think a certain way. That accepted, here is the rub for Western political thought: where does authority reside? Or, as John Dewey observed in *Human Nature and Conflict*, the question of choice arises and the issue of morality comes into existence naturally. Yet even among the most brilliant and compassionate scientists of the last two centuries, the extent to which morality and values are seen to lie outside of nature is but one more example of humankind's mistaken notion that we are ultimately segregated in one very crucial aspect from the entirety of nature.

The idea that morality and values cannot be found in nature is one of the single most erroneous notions Western civilization and modern science have produced and one of the major reasons American Indian students often find science uninviting. Even conceding that nature has indeed equipped humankind with more choice behaviorally than other animals, and certainly plants, this cultural or nurture aspect of human existence is not a repudiation of our natural propensities; rather, it is an affirmation that morality itself is a natural product. It does no good to invoke the old nature-versus-nurture or nature-versus-culture (social) dichotomy, for what it exposes is less valuable than what it obscures: that humankind's heavy dependence on culture, nurturing, or socialization is natural—given by nature.

I would suggest it is more accurate and useful to think of our cultural or social behavior as instinctive, albeit in a nonreductionist manner. In short, human beings have no choice about choice. The invocation of instinct as a product of nature, and morality as a product of culture, is unhelpful when looking at the question of morality, since it in essence assigns nature—the world itself—a mechanical character. It reduces humankind's natural character to instinct—biological mechanism. This reduction of "natural" humans to instinct is not surprising but certainly enlightening, for it again illustrates the extent to which humankind's self-proclaimed moral autonomy from nature is dependent on a reductionism that is at its core mechanical, naively empirical, and teleologically closed—precluding the possibility of change.

Predictably, once the majority of human behavior (that which most humans acknowledge involves choice) is given an autonomous realm or space in which to operate, we enter the postmodernist room full of mirrors, where any attempt to talk about reality or what is real dissolves into digressions on meaning and multiple realities. While I appreciate the postmodernist critique of modernist thought and its unmasking of the arbitrariness of Western civilization, I fundamentally reject its antirealist conclusions. Postmodernists examined modern, essentially Western, theories of the real world, and finding them wanting, simply discarded the phenomenal world and kept theory.

The postmodernist rejection of an objective reality or truth is predictable and well within the intellectual heritage of Western thought. However, its embracing of a purely cultural determination of reality leaves the door open to a cultural relativism and an antire-alist position relative to knowledge. The point missed by modernist theories immersed in the Western tradition and postmodernist theories rebelling against the Western tradition is that both forget their ideas are about something, and that something is experience in the world. Try as humans might to put knowledge in boxes—the experimental method, abstract categories, subjectivistic lockboxes, and so on—we are still left with the large remainder of daily experience. A substantial amount of the wisdom of our indigenous ancestors is still with us in the experience of places too often now taken for granted.

*Power and Place* is a proposal to reflect on critical issues about experience and what we can learn in the larger experiential realm of existence. The issues and questions raised are to a large extent avoided today in formal educational settings: questions about the nature of the world and our human place in the world. They are the important questions, the ones that reductionist science and a Western metaphysics of the world cannot answer. The most fundamental of these questions is, "How shall we live?" and this question is at its core a moral question encompassing power, place, personality, and, ultimately, self-determination.

## INDIGENOUS SELF-DETERMINATION

Indigenous self-determination begins with attentiveness to the relations around us, whether they be typically understood as economic, political, ecological, or spiritual. The everyday experiential world of casinos, manufacturing, so-called natural resource management, and all of the business decisions tribal governments make are central to self-determination. They are central because we are just as free to lose as we are free to choose. We indigenous peoples lose if we make choices without considering the consequences to our unique tribal identities as indigenous peoples emergent from diverse places of this planet. Thankfully, most American Indians still recognize the fact that spiritual questions are inextricably bound up with practical questions, everyday issues, although we may be struggling to make sense of how to meaningfully integrate both when surrounded by a society that so successfully segregates and compartmentalizes human actions and experiences in the world. If all of humankind would seriously undertake to reconnect to places in the practical way their ancestors once did—and many indigenous people still do—we might be much better off.

There is no way to get around the fact that Indian education in America has been and, one might argue, continues to exist as the handmaiden of assimilation. The assimilation of differently minded indigenous people into the dominant, essentially Western Culture, and I mean culture with a big C—the values, beliefs, customs, habits, practices, technology, and languages of Western civilization—has been up to now Indian education. That education is an assimilation process ought to be intrinsically troubling to anyone with democratic values.

I have little problem with people's deciding how to bring their children into their own society and culture. The Pennsylvania Amish maintain their own education system and have even gained the protection of the U.S. Supreme Court to do so. Families have a recognized right within certain guidelines to home-school. In short, democracy suggests people have a right to educate children in accordance with their societal values and beliefs. Why should we expect anything less in our Native communities?

Problems inevitably begin when someone else determines what religion or education ought to be for a particular people's children. In addition, these fundamentally democratic issues become more complicated if groups of people find themselves, for whatever reason, living in a more multicultural human environment. The more heterogeneous the human cultural context, the more difficult it is to declare what core values and beliefs ought to be inculcated through education of children—the future members of a given society. Yet this multicultural reality, more than any argument or ideology, ought to underscore the current challenge in education. Diversity, multicultural society, postmodern critiques of hegemonic, that is, totalizing and universalizing, ideologies—such topics predominate many discussions in education today. The endless debates in and criticism of higher education serve as a de facto demonstration of how pointless this intellectual industry will be unless the debates about curriculum become literally "grounded," contextualized to the environments and places we call home. Human cultures until very recently were emergent out of places; they were literally grounded in the experience of nature in particular places on the planet. If we indigenize or reindigenize self-determination, then it will entail a reordering of values and signal an effort to live in a manner respective of the power, places, and persons surrounding us.

POWER

Power, "the living energy that inhabits and or composes the universe," is what moves us as human beings—all of the connections or relations that form the immediate environment or that small part of the world each of us inhabits. While energy in physical mechanics is quantifiable, Deloria's concept of power is nonquantifiable. Power is a qualitative dimension shaping our thoughts, desires, habits, actions, and institutions that operates to a great extent without us thinking about it. In ordinary language we can call power amorphous, for it takes many forms, some overt and some latent. We are conscious of the former, while the latter lie dormant and have an existence of (to) which we are not initially conscious. We can also describe power as diffuse, for it surrounds us as an *atmosphere of influences*, including the very practical economic influences in the world. Power is quite literally flowing around and into us; if we are properly attentive, power can be used by us.

An indigenous North American metaphysics would agree with the formulation that knowledge is power, but object to the narrow Western idea of knowledge and the anthropocentric, human-centered notion of power. Like the concept of personhood, American Indians and Alaska Natives have a much broader notion of knowledge one that includes knowledge born of direct experience of what I call the atmosphere of influences. Deloria's likening of American Indian metaphysics to a social reality is helpful, for it directs us properly to the character of this atmosphere of influences. Social reality is not what one narrowly thinks of as social; instead, to follow Deloria's suggestion, "social" is as close as we might presently get to describing the substantive character or reality of power. Like society itself, the power allowed as social by most human beings, with the exception of a few intellectuals called methodological individualists, is readily acknowledged in its observable effects. We know society has forces we call social because we experience them and not only see, but also feel, their effects. The nature of social reality has certainly dogged philosophers of science and some serious social scientists. I would suggest that they consider the problem of social reality as only one part of a much larger and more serious exploration of the "nature" of reality in general. To say as Karl Marx first did, and as many sociologists since have said, that we are simultaneously products of and producers of society and history, is a way of saying our human lives are part of a life process we are engaged in—not by choice, but as a consequence of our living existence.

I find it easy to accept that the environment Marx experienced made it relatively simple to see life as a struggle for existence primarily shaped by an economic class struggle. However, it is not romanticism to suggest that Seattle, Ten Bears, Chief Joseph, and many other American Indian leaders of the nineteenth century lived in environments where the notion of a "struggle for existence" never crossed their mind—although concern for living well did. Although it is fashionable today to bash any defense of a tribal aesthetics of cooperation with nature as romantic, I find it difficult to discount the impressions of so many non-Native persons, from conquistadores to Harvard anthropologists, who, in spite of incredibly ethnocentric, if not racist, assessments of our ancestors, all saw indigenous North American societies possessing something they found admirable and lacking in their own Western societies: generosity and a social well-being. Cristobal Colon (Columbus) himself marveled at the goodness of the Taino Indians during his first visit to the Caribbean Islands, and William Howells in *The Heathens* even acknowledged:

American citizens live in an advanced and comfortable nation, yet great numbers of them feel insecure and uncertain, either individually or in groups, to the point of bitter unhappiness. ... Primitive people have long ago put into practical religious forms many things that your countrymen are trying to find for themselves in lectures and books on the good society or how to find happiness or on what is wrong with them.

Good societies, happiness, and individual well-being—or to quote directly from Colon's diary entries of December 24 and December 25, 1492, "They [the Indians] are very gentle and without knowledge of what is evil nor do they murder or steal," and "They love their neighbors as themselves": not bad accomplishments for "savage heathens." Unfortunately, these qualities were not much valued by Colon and many of the Europeans who followed him. The very character of the first interactions between the Caribbean Natives and their strange visitors from Europe remains indicative of the fact that both peoples held very different worldviews. Given what we know of European history, I think most persons would prefer to arrive as strangers at the doorsteps of people like the tribal Taino as opposed to the doorsteps of the civilized Europeans.

We can acknowledge that North America had its own hierarchical states or societies centuries before Cristobol Colon arrived. One of the largest within the geographical boundaries of the present United States, Cahokia, collapsed before A.D. 1100, as did most of the great mound cultures of the Southeast United States and the great Mayan states of Central America. What exactly happened is still open to much research, but in the case of the Mound Builders and the Mayans, I would say, to borrow a popular phrase, "Been there! Done that!" The fact that there seemed no great effort to rebuild these indigenous empires after their collapse suggests to me that some American Indians learned a lesson in self-determination that Western historians embracing a pseudo-evolutionary, or linear, view of world history will find problematic. If, as many North American indigenous worldviews suggest, social organization and culture *ought* to emerge out of our environment—understood as constitutive of an ecological, political and necessarily ethical community—it may be that the earliest state structures in North America demonstrated an incongruity with the environments where they developed. History always occurs in places and never on abstract timelines.

## PLACE

Most American intellectuals and educators continue to talk exclusively about history and cultural issues as if they were disengaged or relatively autonomous from the other features, or as I prefer to acknowledge, the other persons or relatives of our ecological and environmental communities. Much of what I have elaborated in my essays goes back to a three-decades-old insight found in *God Is Red:*

> When the domestic ideology is divided according to American
> Indian and Western European immigrant, however, the funda-
> mental difference is one of great philosophical importance. Ameri-
> can Indians hold their lands—place—as having the highest
> possible meaning, and all their statements are made with this ref-
> erence point in mind.... When one group [American Indian] is
> concerned with the philosophical problem of space and the other
> [Western European immigrant] with the philosophical problem of
> time, the statements of either group do not make much sense
> when transferred from one context to the other without the proper
> consideration of what is happening.

If we seriously add "places" in their ecological, and fundamentally indigenous, sense to the consideration of ideologies, it brings the purely "cultural" problems as conceived by the metaphysics of dominant "American" society into even starker relief. For the cultural wars among those operating in the Western metaphysics of time, space, and energy seem little more than abstract disagreements between antiseptic ideologies—strange visions about human life and culture disengaged or alienated from the land and places.

By reducing success, progress, and self-determination to cut-throat economic measures, we create a Culture (with a big *C*) possessing little value for community among our own species, let alone a broader experience of community, one inclusive of other persons in our immediate world. Deloria is correct to find that meaning in a place is crucial if we are to improve the human condition on this planet, and I believe we will inevitably make progress once we give up the invidious distinctions and dichotomies that have haunted modern Western thought, including nature versus culture (nurture), conservation versus development, and science versus religion (values).

The question of self-determination from the standpoint of an American Indian practice of education is essentially a question of the degree to which individuals and communities are actively engaged in making their future—not in the abstract but in places and in what Dewey called the "lived-in" present. For we are all involved in a living process—some are merely less conscious or, I prefer to say, less aware than others about the future they are enabling through their present activity.

Place or space is concrete and palpable. It is in a profound sense where one discovers his or her self, what Deloria calls personality, as opposed to the casual sense of where one just happens to find one's self. Place is not merely the relationship of things, resources, or objects, it is the site where dynamic processes of interaction occur—where processes between other living beings or other-than-human persons occur. At this point it seems worth noting that history as spatial relations offers a view of change wherein one might think of change as timeless, or at least not time-dependent but space-dependent. Change is understood in a nonmechanistic relational- and process-dependent manner, with processes understood as changes in spatial relations and constellations of power. Thankfully, physics and the life sciences are beginning to acknowledge that the old mechanical and time-dependent view of our lives in this world allowed us to do certain things, manipulate and build things; humans can indeed send people to the moon and have them safely return.

In terms of acting or behaving with a moral intelligence, our human successes have been less than impressive. I believe this is in large part because our pride in controlling/manipulating small "elements" and understanding some processes have made us good at doing some things, but facilitated our losing sight of the big picture and the necessity of asking what things mean. Some will respond, why worry about meaning if one knows how to do things, if one knows how things work? One answer seems incontrovertible: modern or postmodern humankind knows little about how meaning works and consequently little about our human selves.

We live in places today marked by it seems two extremes in human behavior: those who turn almost exclusively inward to find "themselves" and those who define and give meaning to their lives through the outward acquisition of things. One seeks another world in which meaning can be found, and the other decides to literally buy or make his or her world. Both behaviors are odd to tribal persons who find meaning in the world and recognize through experience that they are of a people and place.

PERSONALITY

I understand Deloria's idea of personality as the substantive embodiment, the unique realization, of all the relations and power we embody. Because each of us is someplace and, but for a few exceptions, never in exactly the same place as anybody else, our personalities are unique. Our phenomenal existence entails a spatial dimension and variations in power relations with other persons in the world. Therefore, *personality* as Deloria uses the term is a metaphysical concept, fundamentally different from the popular science view that what and who we are can be reduced to genetics or biochemical mechanisms. In the current reductionist genetic model of "personalities," the critical interaction between environment and personality is all but lost. Even at the most general and abstract level of contemporary evolutionary theory the concept of species masks the uniqueness of individuals.

What I mean can be understood by anyone who has had the long-term friendship of a dog, cat, bird, or "individual" of another species. We (each of us having such a friendship) know our other-than-human person is an individual, different from others of the same kind or breed. Why? Because we know them as persons: we learn through experience their personality. "Pets," however, are a special case given their social circumstances. Anyone attentive to animal groups living outside of human control for an extended period begins to distinguish unique personalities of individuals in the herd or social group. American Indian traditions suggest many of our peoples fully understood how much our own human personalities depended on what could be learned from the other-than-human persons in the world. Our personalities or selves, what Carl Jung called "anima" and Paul Tournier called "persons," as individuals within communities, require this recognition and interaction lest we become merely another demographic minority.

In a world of human-created "virtual" persons, places, and communities, as well as biologically engineered plants and animals, humans seem prepared to become not merely the measure of all things but the creators of the "brave new world" Aldous Huxley foresaw in his cautionary novel by that name. And like Huxley's *Brave New World*, there is one thing missing in the human-created ethernet world of virtual persons and artificial intelligence: a spiritual reality residing in persons and places unmanufactured and not engineered by human-the-creator. A spiritual reality permeates the world we experience, and incredible power exists in places where human creations do not get in the way or become the primary focus of our attention. This is not an argument, as my Comanche friend and colleague Ray Pierotti likes to emphasize, to take humans out of nature or for the maintenance of a pristine wilderness, a Garden of Eden, so to speak. Quite the contrary, it is a declaration that among the atmosphere of influences we move through daily, some powerful and unique influences exist in places not dominated by humankind. One need not read New Age texts to understand this; a survey of the diversity and complexity of distinct human cultures that have existed thus far and are daily threatened proves the point. The world is a diverse and complex reality. The best place to begin an understanding of this reality is with critical reflection regarding our experience. Self-determination requires reflection.

CRITICAL REFLECTION

Self-determination is reflective in two senses. First, in the sense that we can never act consciously until we have arrived at an understanding of who we are—each of us in our own unique place in the world. Here the metaphysics of living in the world draws a clear distinction between itself and the metaphysics of the world whose attendant psychology finds human self-discovery in aesthetic retreat from the world. In many indigenous traditions there are indeed "places" where one might think individuals retreat from the world for reflection and even revelation. Such a conclusion would be false, however, for in these practices the intention is not escape from the world but to seek out a better connection in the world, a connection to influences—power—that cannot be casually acquired. Heightened awareness of this/these power(s) does indeed require self-conscious reflection; however, reflection, or even contemplation, is not focused on some abstract or ideal sense of self but, if you will, on a process of discovery.

And it is this process of discovery that brings us to the second reflective feature of the question of self-determination: the focus of our attention is to the relations and connections that influence who we are and are constitutive of our being, or what Deloria calls personality. Tribal traditions were not guided by a formal rule of law but by custom and habit. Browning Pipestem once asked Haskell students, "What is 'the law'?" After they struggled mightily with the question, he gave an excellent answer and one illustrative of indigenous traditions: "The law," he said with a pause, "is a contract—an agreement—between strangers." Modern legal theory, in fact the law, is to a large extent an abstract human construction. However, and here is the critical point, in modern societies and nation-states, it is necessarily more meaningfully congruent with vague ideologies than customs, habits, and ceremonies in a land-based community of persons we know—experientially. Modern law is quite literally no respecter of real persons, but a definer and defender of persons in the abstract. That human beings in modern legal theories are philosophical constructions is an ex post facto demonstration that persons constructing laws no longer share an experiential place, as well as a demonstration of the evaporation of culture emergent from a place. In an indigenous practice of education informed by an experiential metaphysics, the focus of self-determination is on the manner in which our being and identity itself is constituted of the number of good relationships we are part of and actively maintain. Self-determination cannot be an individual question, for the reflective sense in which our selves are grounded in life among our relations and in the relationships surrounding us requires engagement with the community of persons, both human and other-than-human, when we determine what we ought to do, what choices we should make, and how we should be self-determining.

Such a notion is indeed complex if left entirely to rational calculation, but experience gives us a source for estimation that goes beyond rational calculation. Self-determination in the dominant Western society is essentially about calculation, and appropriately so, for it has emerged in a legal culture of abstractions, of abstract persons, with abstract rights or freedoms. In such a model of politics—law, rights, responsibilities (of which there are few, for the most part), and power—solving political questions is like solving a problem in mathematics, given the right terms and operations. Legal constructionists, sympathetic to the points made above, get quickly frustrated, for in acknowledging the complexity of political environments as experienced, they quickly give up on rational elaboration of such complex models. To use an analogy from the quantitative social sciences, once one factors in more than a couple of independent variables in a computer-generated regression model of causal variables, the interaction effects are such that it grows increasingly difficult to say precisely what the effect of any single variable is. Rational calculation gets interminably difficult and hence, so the argument goes, impractical. I could not agree more.

However, the problem is solved once one gives up on calculation and abstraction and instead redirects attention to experience through custom, habit, ceremony, and what I choose to call the development of a synthetic attentiveness. By synthetic attentiveness I mean a heightened sense of awareness that operates without thinking about it or paying attention to it. Synthetic attentiveness is the "I experience, therefore I am" indigenous response to Descartes's famous "I think, therefore I am." I have seen this keen awareness or synthetic attentiveness operate numerous times with traditional elders who demonstrate the amazing ability to be aware of events, processes, and activities surrounding them that most of us miss. Whether visiting a classroom, having a meeting with governmental officials, or being in wetlands or on a grassland prairie, I have often been surprised in discussions afterward by what these elders "noticed" without seeming to notice at all. This ability to what I will call process processes is not magical, and it only seems mysterious to those insistent on a rational schematic or mechanistic model to explain what happens. I can offer neither. I see no need to; rather, this processing of processes seems acquired by paying attention—by learning to be attentive to the world we live in.

The question of self-determination is one of degree: how engaged, connected, and attentive are we to our community? This will seem contradictory and paradoxical to Western-thinking students and teachers. The more attentive one is to their community, the more self-determining they can be; the less attentive, the more selfish and self-destructing they will be. Christopher Lasch struck a chord with many in his description of Western culture, and contemporary American culture in particular, as a *Culture of Narcissism*—a culture of self-love. I would merely extend Lasch's insightful commentary to the love of all things or objects embodying selfishness.

## METAPHYSICS FOR LIVING

Indigenous metaphysics offers insights into many of the most troubling problems modern or postmodern societies face, by recognizing the world as having living physical and spiritual dimensions, not as a fast and fixed thing. Space, places, ecosystems, and environments are not the "final frontier" waiting to be conquered and controlled by modern ideologies; rather, they constitute the context through which we escape the abstract relativism of postmodernist thought and find what it means to be self-determining.

American Indian metaphysics has the advantage of framing all questions of knowledge as fundamentally moral questions that literally reside in our everyday life. The way many of us live today makes it easy to compartmentalize different aspects of our life. The strength that Deloria has always found in American Indian metaphysics is their emergence from a way of life. As we think about what it means to exercise self-determination, we must *not avoid* examining so-called economic, political, and social aspects of our lives as part of larger moral questions and what it means to be indigenous today. It may very well be as the elder Dan in *Neither Wolf Nor Dog* told Kent Nerburn: living with honor is just as important, if not more important, than living with freedom. We are obsessed with freedoms, but freedom to do what? If we fail to ask these foundational questions in education, it seems disingenuous to complain about behavior later. So let us think about self-determination indigenously: about what living with honor means to Peoples still connected to places.

# THE PERPETUAL
# EDUCATION REPORT

*V. Deloria*

*This essay was originally written in 1992 at the beginning of the*
*Clinton Administration. We never did hear very much about that*
*educational report, and, after a fancy gathering in New Mexico at the*
*start of Clinton's term, we never did hear much about anything. Now*
*we have a new administration and—we can easily predict—a new*
*education report.*

In authorizing the report the secretary of education is following an
age-old and revered tradition in Indian education: It is better to
talk about education than to educate. The ink will hardly be dry
on this report before another organization, or another federal
agency, has the urge to investigate, and the cycle will begin again.
From the Reverend Jedidiah Morse in the 1820s through Senator
Kennedy to the present, the refrain is the same: "We are not doing
anything, we need more money, and Indians need to be involved."

Why is it that, in spite of sincerity oozing from every pore in
their bodies, investigators of Indian education reach the same dull,
stifling, and uncreative conclusions? Educational professionals
argue that the problems are always the same, that the federal government never has adequately funded its educational branches, and
consequently each report is basically dealing with past and existing
inadequacies. I don't buy it. Big-city school superintendents give
the same argument, and when you give them additional funds, they
add an incredible number of bureaucrats, cut classroom budgets,

dress up a few motivational programs, and begin laying the groundwork for a new bond issue. That Washington educators would do less is difficult to believe. Graduate schools of education across the nation teach these people that abusing the taxpayer is their *only* function.

The second most popular argument in Indian education is that Indians are really a different cultural set and therefore generate different kinds of problems. Cultural differences should have been reasonably clear in 1492 and by the early 1700s when formal educational efforts for Indians began. Someone should have started to think about what cultural difference meant. Certainly after almost three centuries people ought to be getting a grip on the nature of this cultural difference. But now, after 500-plus years of European contact, it should not come as any surprise that Indians really do represent an entirely different set of cultural beliefs and practices, even though many of the most profound differences have disappeared over the last century.

Each education report concludes with the proposition that the government has to do more to get Indians involved in education. In some instances involvement means organization of parent advisory groups, at other times Indian school boards; and occasionally we are told that it is sufficient to scold Indian parents so that they will act like white parents, a good many of whom are more delinquent than all the Indians put together. In practice, Indian involvement usually means bringing a large crowd of Indians together so they can listen to a panel of educators tell them that they should become more involved in education.

If there really are profound cultural differences, if Indian parents should be more involved in their children's education, and if more funds should be spent, what is it that dooms reform efforts when minimal programs are devised to meet these perceived needs? The thing that has always been missing in Indian education, and is still missing today, is Indians. In spite of the many advisory committees, national organizations, and graduate programs in education that purport to deal specifically with Indian education, we see nary a trace of Indianness in either efforts or results.

Such an argument must certainly offend the many Indians who serve on these committees and work in national educational organizations, but the truth is that when they join these groups and take on these responsibilities, they generally leave their Indian heritage behind and adopt the vocabulary and concepts of non-Indian educators and bureaucrats, following along like so many sheep. There is some sincerity in their efforts. Many of them feel that in adopting the technical language of modern education they are making Indian needs relevant to influential people who can help turn Indian education around. The sad fact is that in modern American education, frenetic activity is mistaken for ability and capability.

Indians do play an inhibiting role in the development of new ideas in education by insisting that any policy-making group have an Indian membership. This demand goes far back into the early 1960s, when it was necessary to insist on some Indian representation in the many task forces and investigating committees that were being formed to work on Indian poverty. But it is necessarily a useless concept and fruitless requirement if the Indians who are being appointed fail to represent Indian interests. A committee composed entirely of Indians who parrot the educational party line is perhaps worse than a committee composed wholly of non-Indians who have some glimmer of what problems are and how they can be addressed. Let us take the three identifiable issues, cultural difference, family involvement, and funding problems, and discuss how these concepts should be used to support changes in Indian education.

CULTURAL DIFFERENCES

So many cultural differences exist between Indians and non-Indians that almost any cultural trait can be chosen to illustrate possible changes. For our purposes we will take the continuously observed fact that Indians are not competitive. This argument is not to say that Indians never compete but rather that aggressive public demonstrations of competition are regarded as crude behavior. American education is designed to encourage people to compete with their peer group and measures individuals against each other. The system taken as a whole relies heavily upon the experiences and values of the middle class, and consequently test scores are based upon the worldviews that mainstream Protestant Americans believe to be true, whether they are in fact or not. Teachers frequently cite the lack of Indian competitiveness as a detriment to learning and seek ways to overcome Indian children's shyness.

If we really understood cultural differences and developed our educational programs to build upon the strengths of each culture, teachers would not be concerned with overcoming shyness, they would build on it. One need only read Charles Eastman's book *Indian Boyhood* to see how Indians handled peer-group pressures in education. The boys were asked to choose which of the birds was the best mother and were given time to formulate their answers. Each boy chose an appropriate characteristic of bird behavior and motherly concerns, made his argument, and was prepared to turn aside other evidence. Discussion was lively, something that would make any modern teacher envious, and each answer given was a sophisticated blending of the knowledge of birds and the interpretation of their behavior using human analogs. In a sense this was competition between the boys in picking the proper bird. In a larger sense, each boy's reasoning was given a measure of respect as he did demonstrate that he had chosen reasonable virtues from among the many he could identify.

Tribal elders today teach a good many techniques and tribal history using the same methods of instruction, and almost every comprehensive book on tribal histories and culture will have some space devoted to tribal teaching practices. Consequently, there is no excuse for avoiding traditional ways of teaching in favor of non-Indian techniques that have proven themselves failures. Using either the oral traditions or some of the written materials that are available, it would not be difficult to reconstitute a class of Indian children and instruct them in much more efficient ways. Storytelling with the further requirement of being able to recite the story accurately after hearing it several times would make the accumulation of knowledge fun again.

The Indian view of the world tends to see unities both in the structure of physical things and in the behavior of things, and we have recently been describing it as "holistic" in that it tries to present a comprehensive picture in which the parts and their value are less significant than the larger picture and its meaning. That is not to say that Indians could not deal with specific items of knowledge. Most Indian languages have a multitude of words to describe phenomena, and Indian words can easily be arranged to provide new words and concepts. In fact, Indian language can achieve more precision than English, even while conveying the emotional nuances necessary to make knowledge come alive and remain with the person.

Look at the curriculum that Indian children are asked to use. Knowledge of the world is divided up into separate categories that seem to be completely isolated from each other. So profound is this separation that most children, Indian and non-Indian, rebel when they are asked to write complete sentences in classes other than English, or to show any comprehension of mathematics in any course except mathematics and physics/engineering. We are asking children to divide the world into predetermined categories of explanation and training them to avoid seeing the complete picture of what is before their eyes. Efforts of the last three decades have been somewhat bizarre when this question is faced directly. Quite often the images familiar to Indians are used instead of traditional white, middle-class images, and this change in pictorial representation is supposed to cure the defect in the child's perspective. If the child wants to understand the whole, we simply dress up the parts in buckskin and pretend that we have answered the problem.

FAMILY INVOLVEMENT

The original intent of Indian education was to wean the child away from his or her family, community, relatives, clan, band, and tribe. People seriously believed that if an Indian child was brought within the purview of non-Indian education at an early age, the corruptive influences of Indian people would not affect them and they would grow up to be "normal." That is to say, they would naturally adopt and exemplify all the values and perspectives of the non-Indian society. I remember meeting a high-level educator in the 1970s who was absolutely convinced that Navajo children would have automatically spoken English if they had been anywhere else than the reservation. These attitudes, while not completely eliminated, changed profoundly after the Meriam Report, which gave emphasis to building programs on the basis of what actually existed in the reservation communities.

If family involvement is so important, why is it that developments in the past four decades have made it impossible to connect the family and the school? During the New Deal there was a great emphasis on the reservation day schools. These schools were located wherever there was a significant concentration of people on the reservations, and they serviced a small population, often in one-room schoolhouses. Teachers lived in the local communities and knew the parents, grandparents, and families and participated in all local activities. Indeed, the schoolhouse, no matter how insignificant, was the center of local social activity. Families felt they were part of education because everyone who had anything to do with the schooling of their children was an important part of their community.

Today we have monstrously large school plants that resemble nothing so much as prisons. Indian children ride buses for hours each day to attend school. The enrollment in large consolidated schools is so big that discipline becomes a problem, and school activities, while certainly more plentiful and attractive, become exercises in mass movement. Large schools require an immense administrative staff, most of whom spend their time pushing forms from one desk to another or attending conferences to learn how to make administration even more complicated. Indian children are lost in these gigantic institutions, and to survive, we now see them organizing gangs on reservations. We have imported the urban environment; we have not brought education to the reservation at all.

For the past twenty years there has been a big emphasis on getting parents involved with this educational machine. Both the tribes and federal educators have preached PTA and parent activities, and advisory committees on various programs and activities of the school have blossomed like runaway zucchini. With some rare exceptions, no provisions have been made to include grandparents and uncles and aunts, the people who traditionally took responsibility for much of the children's education. PTAs and other parent groups have been organized using entirely artificial criteria, primarily residence within a certain geographical area—as if people shared some mysterious social cement by geography alone.

The psychological burden of even attending a meeting in a big, formal, brick building is intimidating to many reservation parents. It calls back memories of their childhood and the summons to come to the agency, which always meant problems. Families are herded through large school plants every year at "welcome back to school" days, but the format used, the quick tour with smiling teachers defending their classroom doors, makes it clear to parents that they are outsiders and are not to appear at the school unless they are asked. Multiply this feeling by several thousand and you can experience the feelings of the Indian child the first several weeks of school.

The presence of consolidated schools makes reform in this area a difficult proposition at the present time. Changes in the educational system are probably dependent upon corresponding and prior changes in the tribal governments that vest more self-governing powers in local communities. In fact, the major reform that needs to be made on many reservations is a change of perceptions about what tribes and reservations are. They should be understood in their national character, which is to say, as instrumentalities expressing the national existence of the people and dealing with primarily outside forces and entities. Local communities should take on the characteristics of municipalities and formal village institutions that include local control of education and social activities.

Wherever possible local communities should begin to take control of primary and part of secondary education, even if it starts in one-room schoolhouses. Local control should emphasize control over curriculum, with teaching about tribal history, tribal customs and traditions, and tribal language at the earliest possible age with maximum use of traditional people. The activity should be perceived as Indian or tribal. This emphasis is in contrast to the present orientation, which is that the participants are Indian, but that the kinds of activities they are asked to support are basically non-Indian in origin. A considerable part of the school activities, particularly including much of the testing, should be transformed into social/educational events of the community. When the Five Civilized Tribes operated their own school system, they used to have several days of formal recitation of what students had learned or were learning in school, and the communities played an integral role in judging whether or not the school system was educating their children.

We need not project futuristic plans that may never become feasible. A good way to begin involving families and communities would be to introduce two subjects to Indian primary and secondary education: family genealogies and tribal traditions. These two subjects provide a solid foundation for children's personal identity as well as serving as a context for teaching all manner of social skills and development of memory and recollection. In a world of large institutional restraints, knowledge of family and tribe would provide a significant set of skills to provide confidence in the child that he or she is part of an ongoing human experience. The best possible setting in which these kinds of teaching can take place is informally outside the school building, using a conversational method of instruction. If Indians presently involved in Indian education would but stop and think of their own knowledge of the world, they would realize that while they cannot remember anything of what they were taught in grade school, they have instant and highly accurate recall of stories they heard elders tell several decades ago in informal, casual settings.

FUNDING PROBLEMS

If ever there was a school superintendent who thought he or she had sufficient funds to operate during the school year, the world would have come to an end. Federal bureaucrats can stand in the midst of incredibly wasteful expenditures and weep real tears about how inadequately they are funded. In addition to outright squandering of resources on administrative perks, conferences, and research projects, the federal Indian education budget reflects the contemporary institutional configuration on the reservations and in state school districts—neither of which allocates funds on a sensible basis. Funds derived from Johnson-O'Malley, PL 874, and the Indian Education Act are all seen as supplemental to existing state, local, and federal programs and budgets. Consequently, everything in the funding area is oblique to the purpose of education and is designed not specifically to educate Indians, but to ensure that the Bureau of Indian Affairs and local non-Indian school districts prosper. If Indian children happen to get an education in the process, fine.

With large consolidated schools, budgets reflect the size of the plant and operations, with teaching a minor component in the overall scheme of things. It is difficult to get national figures on various specific items of expenditure, but it would not be surprising if there were one administrator and/or staff person for each teacher actually in the classroom. With the increasing shortage of oil escalating the cost of fuel, busing children will now substantially distort the expenses of every school serving Indian children. It is impossible to estimate the cost of heating and cooling large buildings as opposed to smaller schoolhouses, but the differences must be significant.

Included in the funding area, although only of related importance, is the incredible amount of money being spent on various kinds of research in Indian education, including special supplementary programs of enrichment. With the exception of California and a few school districts scattered across the country, it is possible for a person to get a degree in "education," taking courses that are essentially method and theory classes in education, and having minimal course work in the subjects that are actually going to be taught. These credits are frequently survey courses that give a minimum knowledge of the subject. When these teachers try to teach students, they discover they have such a sparse background that it is nearly impossible to hold students' interest. Thus, the cry goes out for better textbooks and curriculum. The problem is not the curriculum but the inadequate training of the teacher. So countless dollars are spent in research on curriculum, when better teacher educational requirements are actually needed.

Finally, the politics should be taken out of Indian education funding, particularly in the Title IV funds. It is not difficult to look at the Title IV awards, compare them with the politics of NACIE and NIEA—which have been the two leading Indian organizations involved in making educational policy as part of the movement toward self-determination in education—and understand what is happening. And a glance at the various universities that perennially receive large educational grants, but produce few graduates, will show the interfacing of the Indian and non-Indian educational old-boy network. The shifting of personnel within the Bureau of Indian Affairs school system will also provide a means of tracking Indian political decisions. As long as Indian education is a function of Indian national politics, we should not hear Indian educators complain too loudly about the failures of the federal government in this field.

A good argument can be made that the Indian educational network is now so entrenched that no reforms are possible. During the past three decades we have seen an endless parade of people occupy the major positions in Indian education. We are now at the point where we are recycling people—if the latest appointments are any indication of the state of affairs. Why is it that after nearly twenty-five years of producing Indian educational administrators, the short list for appointments always looks like the bimbo finalist list?

We define the problem in education as originating in the difference in cultural outlook. If this observation is really true, why do we have educators put in charge of correcting the problem? It might be far better to appoint a well-trained humanist instead of a recycled Indian politician. For all the fanfare we have had about putting Indians in charge of the bureau and Indian education, the best people we have seen in policy-making positions have been John Collier, a bohemian social worker, and Philleo Nash, a renegade anthropologist. There is much to be said about putting someone in charge who knows about people and not another person who can manipulate rules and regulations to the satisfaction of Indian political cliques.

Indian education doesn't need another shallow report. In view of the impending collapse of American institutions, such as the family farm, local banks, and the housing market, it would appear that our society will be undergoing major disruptive changes for the next several decades. Because about half of the Indians live on the reservations, it may be necessary to move to some kind of subsistence economy if the people are going to survive the upcoming economic catastrophe. The financial choices in Indian education will become apparent. We will either continue to operate existing school systems with declining funds or start to make fundamental changes in how we educate children and allocate resources to do so.

Instead of boring us with another tedious recital of the failure of the federal government to educate Indians—which is embarrassingly obvious—the secretary of education would do well to find some way to confront the reality of Indian culture, community, and history and devise an educational program to meet this specific challenge. If traditional institutions, programs, and teaching have to be changed, so be it. After five centuries of contact, it does not seem too much to ask non-Indian educators and institutions to come to grips with the reality that is the American Indian.

# BIBLIOGRAPHY

Alliance for Childhood, Fool's Gold: A Critical Look at Computers. College Park, Maryland: Alliance for Childhood, 2000.

Basso, Keith, *Wisdom Sits In Places: Landscape & Language among the Western Apache.* Albuquerque: University of New Mexico Press, 1996

Bennett, William, *The Moral Compass: Stories for a Life's Journey.* New York: Simon & Schuster, 1995.

Bridgman, Percy W., *The Way Things Are.* Ann Arbor, Michigan: Bell and Howell Information and Learning, 1959.

Cajete, Gregory, *Look to the Mountain.* Skylamd, North Carolina: Kivaki Press, 1993.

Dawkins, Richard, *The Selfish Gene.* New York: Oxford University Press, 1989.

Deloria, Vine Jr., *We Talk, You Listen: New Tribes, New Turf.* New York: MacMillan. 1970.

———, *God Is Red.* New York: Grosset & Dunlap, 1973.

———, *The Metaphysics of Modern Existence.* New York: Harper & Row, 1979.

———, *Spirit & Reason: The Vine Deloria Jr. Reader.* Golden, Colorado: Fulcrum Publishing, 1999.

DesCartes, Rene, *Discourse on Method and Meditations on First Philosophy.* Indianapolis, Indiana:Hackett Publishing, 1978.

Dewey, John, *Human Nature and Conduct: An introduction to social psychology.* New York: Modern Library, 1957.

Eastman, Charles, Indian Boyhood. New York: Dover, 1971.

Ellul, Jacques, *The Technological Society.* New York: Vintage Books, 1964.

Fowler, H.W., *A Dictionary of Modern English Usage.* New York: Oxford University Press, 1952.

Howells, William, *The Heathen's: Primitive Man and His Religion.* Garden City: New York: Doubleday., 1948.

Hume, David, *An Enquirey Concerning Human Understanding.* New York: Oxford University Press, 1999.

Huxley, Aldous, *Brave New World.* New York: Bantam, 1966.

James, William, *Varieties of Religious Experience.* New York: Doubleday, 1978.

Jung, C.G., *The Development of Personality*. Princeton, New Jersey: Princeton University Press, 1981.

Kant, Immanuel, *Pepetual Peace and Other Essays*. Indianapolis, Indiana: Hackett Publishing, 1983.

Lasch, Christopher, *The Culture of Narcissism: American Life in an Age of Diminishing Expectations*. New York: W.W. Norton, 1979.

Locke, John, *Second Treatise of Government*. Indianapolis, Indiana: Hackett Publishing, 1980.

Lovelock, J.E., *Gaia: A New Look at Life on Earth*. New York: Oxford University Press, 1979.

McKeon, Richard P., *Introduction to Aristotle*. (Modern Library Series) New York: Random House. 1992.

Marx, Karl and Frederick Engels, *The German Ideology*. Moscow, Russia: Progress Publishers, 1976.

Mohawk, John, "Animal Nations Right To Survive," *Daybreak*, 1988.

Morrison, Samuel Eliot,ed., *Journals and Other Documents on the Life and Voyages of Columbus*. New York: Heritage, 1963.

Nerburn, Kent, *Neither Wolf nor Dog: On Forgotten Roads with an Indian Elder*. Novato, California: New World, 1994.

Sagan, Carl, *Billions And Billions: Thpughts on Life and Death at the Brink of the Millennium*. New York: Random House, 1997.

Sale, Kirkpatrick, *The Conquest of Paradise*. New York: Alfred A. Knopf, 1991.

Steiner, Stan, *The New Indians*. New York: Dell, 1968.

Suzuki,David and Peter Knudtson, *Wisdom of the Elders: Honoring Sacred Native Visions of Nature*. New York: Bantam Books, 1993.

Thomas, Elizabeth Marshall, *The Tribe of Tiger: Cats & Their Culture*. New York: Simon & Schuster, 1994.

Tinker, George, "Religion," *Encyclopedia of North American Indians*, Frederick Hoxie, ed. New York: Houghton, 1996.

Tocqueville, Alexis de, *Democracy in America*, Richard D Heffner ed. New York: Mentor, 1956.

Will, George and George Hyde, *Corn Among the Indians of the Upper Mississippi*. Lincoln, Nebraska: University of Nebraska Press, 1976.

Wilson, E. 0., "Integrated Science and the Coming Century of the Environment," *Science*, 1988.

# INDEX

*Note: f. indicates figure.*

Adamson, Rebecca, 16
Administration, 125
Alliance for Childhood, 76–77
American Indian knowledge. See also Knowledge
   of animals, 24–25
   correlation, 26–27
   emphasis on the particular, 22
   information by observation, 27
   of the natural world, 1–2, 21–22, 36
   of plants, 25
   realism of, 27–28
   and respect, 21–22
   of the stars, 21, 25–26
American Indian metaphysics, 49. See also American
   Indian knowledge
   as basis for expansion of contemporary thought,
     98–99
   as basis for living well, 52
   compared with Aristotle's philosophy, 92–99, 96f.
   extension of personality, 93–94
   holistic worldview, 8, 12–13, 16–17, 124–127, 155
   and indigenous worldviews, 39
   reconstructing traditional understanding, 51–52
   and self-determination, 149–150
   value of traditional ways, 8–9
   and western science, 1–6, 30–31
American Indian Religious Freedom Act, 49
American Indian students
   disorientation resulting from differing cultural val-
     ues, 114, 115
   and Federal policy, 102–103
   and science, 27–28, 42, 81–82, 130–132
   as scouts, 109
   and traditional ways, 59, 64–65
American Indians
   application of scientific knowledge to tribal issues,
     130–132
   collapse of pre-Columbian hierarchical societies, 142
   and degeneration of Western culture, 129
   and education as indoctrination, 42, 133
   generosity and social well-being, 141–142
   intellectual comparison of Indian and Western be-
     liefs, 132–133
   and religious freedom, 48–49
   revival of traditional practices, 46
   and shortcomings of professional knowledge,
     125–127
   spirituality, not religion, 53–54
   traditional education, 43–45, 79–80
   understanding Western culture, 18–19
Amish, 139
Anima, 146
Animals, 24–25, 44–45
   languages of, 59–60
   traditional technology of, 58–59
Annette, Cynthia, 72
Anomalies, 21, 63–64

Appaloosa, 58
Appropriateness, 23–24, 25
Aristotle, 10, 88
   on community and diversity, 95
   compared with indigenous thought, 92–99, 96f.
   naturalism, 91
   politics and ethics, 89–92
   and the state, 90, 91–92
   summum bonum, 88, 90, 92, 96f.
Bacon, Francis, 97
Balance, 63–64
Basso, Keith, 75
Beans, 25
Bennett, William, 9
Big Brother, 17
Big Dipper, 26
Billions and Billions, 7
Biological diversity, 37
Black Elk, 6
Bows, 59
Braa, Dean, 136
Brave New World, 146
Bridgman, Percy W., 22
Buffalo, 25
Buffalo Dance, 24
Bureau of Indian Affairs, 106, 109, 159
Bush, George, 107
Cahokia, 142
Causality, 50–51
Cherokees, 35, 104–105
Child development, 13
Clan systems, 34–35, 60–61
   and personality, 93–94
Clinton, Bill, 107, 151
Collier, John, 160
Colon, Cristobal, 37, 54–55, 141–142
Colonialism, 37–38
Columbus, Christopher. See Colon, Cristobal
Communications, 72–73
Community, 28, 72–73, 96f.. See also Clan systems,
   Family, TC3
   rootlessness of mainstream society, 84
Community service, 118–119
Competition, 153–154
The Conquest of Paradise, 54–55
Conspicuous consumption, 70
Corn, 25
Corn Dances, 24
Correlation, 26–27
Creation stories, 60–61
Cultural differences, 152–155, 160
Cultural diversity, 37–38
Culture, 72–73. See also American Indians, TC3,
   Western culture
Dakota, 72
Dams, 71–72
Dawkins, Richard, 11

165